Social Issues
in Literature

Death in Ernest Hemingway's *The Old Man and the Sea*

Other Books in the Social Issues in Literature Series:

Social Issues in Literature

Death in Ernest Hemingway's *The Old Man and the Sea*

Dedria Bryfonski, Book Editor

GREENHAVEN PRESS
A part of Gale, Cengage Learning

GALE
CENGAGE Learning·

Farmington Hills, Mich • San Francisco • New York • Waterville, Maine
Meriden, Conn • Mason, Ohio • Chicago

Elizabeth Des Chenes, *Director, Content Strategy*
Cynthia Sanner, *Publisher*
Douglas Dentino, *Manager, New Product*

© 2014 Greenhaven Press, a part of Gale, Cengage Learning

WCN: 01-100-101

For more information, contact:
Greenhaven Press
27500 Drake Rd.
Farmington Hills, MI 48331-3535
Or you can visit our Internet site at gale.cengage.com

Articles in Greenhaven Press anthologies are often edited for length to meet page requirements. In addition, original titles of these works are changed to clearly present the main thesis and to explicitly indicate the author's opinion. Every effort is made to ensure that Greenhaven Press accurately reflects the original intent of the authors. Every effort has been made to trace the owners of copyrighted material.

Cover image © adoc-photos/Corbis.

LIBRARY OF CONGRESS CATALOGING-IN-PUBLICATION DATA

Death in Ernest Hemingway's The old man and the sea / Dedria Bryfonski, book editor.
    pages cm. -- (Social Issues in Literature)
    Includes bibliographical references and index.
    ISBN 978-0-7377-6978-4 (hardback) -- ISBN 978-0-7377-6979-1 (paperback)
    1. Hemingway, Ernest, 1899-1961. Old man and the sea. 2. Death in literature.
    3. Mortality in literature. I. Bryfonski, Dedria editor of compilation. II. Title.
    PS3515.E37O5215 2014
    813'.52--dc23
                                                                    2013033390

Printed in Mexico
1 2 3 4 5 6 7 18 17 16 15 14

Contents

Chapter 1: Background on Ernest Hemingway

It is difficult to distinguish Hemingway the person from Hemingway the writer because he so often wrote about his own experiences and emotions. *The Old Man and the Sea* is an example of this overlap. Both Santiago the fisherman and Hemingway the writer are in the twilight of their years, facing severe adversity in the pursuit of their crafts.

Hemingway was profoundly self-destructive and the effects of his escapades severely damaged his body and mind by the time he was sixty. With his memory and ability to write destroyed by electroshock treatments for depression, Hemingway committed suicide. His death continues to fascinate people.

Hemingway's good friend and biographer recalls that he dismissed Hemingway's insistence that the Federal Bureau of Investigation (FBI) was spying on him as irrational paranoia. Several decades later, A.E. Hotchner learned that the FBI did indeed have Hemingway under surveillance, and he believes this harassment may have contributed to the writer's suicide.

Chapter 2: *The Old Man and the Sea* and Death

Death is typically presented as arbitrary and violent in Hemingway's earlier stories. In *The Old Man and the Sea*, death is no longer viewed as fearful for those with an understanding of the interconnectedness of nature.
The inevitability of death is a major motif in the works of Hemingway, and all of his major characters suffer life-threatening wounds. Santiago is the most fully realized Hemingway hero—a man who struggles in solitude against the forces of nature and death.

In Hemingway's worldview, violence and death are an integral part of the harmony of nature, with each living being having a role to play based on the being's natural instincts. The heroic figure takes greater risks, making him more vulnerable to defeat and death.

Although many of Hemingway's works deal with death, it was only in his last three books, including *The Old Man and the Sea*, that he wrote about a man struggling with the knowledge of imminent death. Santiago has a task he must complete before the end of his life.

During the last years of his life, Hemingway was concerned with how to confront his own approaching old age and death. In *The Old Man and the Sea*, Hemingway romanticizes old age—Santiago is mythic in his courage and resilience.

Chapter 3: Contemporary Perspectives on Death

There is no reason for those who do not believe in an afterlife to fear death. As the Greek philosopher Epicurus taught, when death occurs, one ceases to exist, and it is pointless to be concerned about something one will not experience.

Young people who have negative thoughts about aging are more likely to engage in risky behaviors related to sexual activity, drinking, tobacco use, and drug abuse that can lead to an early death. These negative thoughts, such as ageism and anxiety about death, could possibly be reduced by special programs.

Introduction

Ernest Hemingway had the singular experience of being able to offer a rebuttal to his own obituary. In January 1954, while on safari in Africa, Hemingway and his wife, Mary, barely survived two small plane crashes along the Nile River one day apart. A search airplane flying over the wreckage of the first crash reported there were no survivors, causing newspapers around the world to print obituaries of Hemingway. In her memoir *How It Was*, Mary Welsh Hemingway relates that her husband obsessively read and reread those obituaries while recovering in a Nairobi hotel room. Reflecting on the experience in the article "A Christmas Gift" for *Look* magazine, Hemingway wrote:

> "In all obituaries, or almost all, it was emphasized that I had sought death all my life. Can one imagine that if a man sought death all of his life he could not have found her before the age of 54? . . . She is the most easy thing to find that I know of. . . . [I have spent my] life avoiding death as cagily as possible, but on the other hand taking no backchat from her and studying her as you would a beautiful harlot who could put you soundly to sleep forever."

By that account, Hemingway seemed to be in command of the situation, far from morbid, with a seasoned, well-adjusted attitude toward the eventual end of a man's life. Yet journalists had ample reasons to speculate that Hemingway, who ended his own life with a double-barreled shotgun on the morning of July 2, 1961, possessed a death wish. In his *Hemingway: A Biography*, Jeffrey Meyers includes an appendix listing the writer's accidents and illnesses—including thirty-two separate injuries, ranging from those suffered in battle and sports to car accidents. The evidence of all this trauma, often following self-risking decisions, has led family members, acquaintances, and literary critics to speculate about the source of Hemingway's preoccupation with death and whether or not he had a death wish.

According to Meyers, Hemingway's obsession with death began early.

> Suicide was a recurrent theme in Hemingway's life and work. Even before his father's suicide in 1928, which profoundly influenced his ideas and emotions, he was obsessed by the theme of self-destruction. Marcelline [Hemingway's older sister] recalled that the young Ernest liked to read [Robert Louis] Stevenson's *The Suicide Club* (an appropriate name for the Hemingway family). As he was recovering from his war wound in October 1918, he expressed a belief that he held till the end of his life: "How much better . . . to go out in a blaze of light, than to have your body worn out and old and illusions shattered."

Meyers argues that Hemingway's suicide was a natural extension of a life lived on the edge.

> There was . . . an existential element in his suicide. His code—formulated in youth, based on toughness and stoicism—was not suited to old age and failed him at the end. . . . His death—a sudden, passionate, violent self-extinction—was perfectly consistent with his life.

Not all people in a position to know agreed. Taking a cue from the writer, Hemingway's biographer and good friend A.E. Hotchner discounted the popular theory of a death wish. In "A Hero, Removed: A.E. Hotchner on Hemingway's Role as 'Emissary of Other Men's Dreams,'" Hotchner contended, "What he was really looking for was to have a hell of a good time every day of his life." A differing view was posed by psychiatrist Christopher D. Martin in "Ernest Hemingway: A Psychological Autopsy of a Suicide," in the winter 2006 issue of *Psychiatry* magazine. Based on his review of biographies, psychiatric literature, personal correspondence, photography, and medical records, Martin arrived at the following diagnosis:

Significant evidence exists to support the diagnoses of bipolar disorder, alcohol dependence, traumatic brain injury, and probable borderline and narcissistic personality traits. Late in life, Hemingway also developed symptoms of psychosis likely related to his underlying affective illness and superimposed alcoholism and traumatic brain injury. Hemingway utilized a variety of defense mechanisms, including self-medication with alcohol, a lifestyle of aggressive, risk-taking sportsmanship, and writing, in order to cope with the suffering caused by the complex co-morbidity of his interrelated psychiatric disorders. Ultimately, Hemingway's defense mechanisms failed, overwhelmed by the burden of his complex co-morbid illness, resulting in his suicide.

Martin suggests two childhood experiences traumatized Hemingway and were at the root of his psychosis—one involving his controlling mother and the other involving his bullying father. Although it was the fashion to dress infants alike in feminine frocks, Grace Hemingway continued outfitting her young son in lacy dresses for longer than would be considered normal. Through most of his adult life, Hemingway referred to his mother as "that bitch." The other parent, Clarence Hemingway, was a strict disciplinarian who beat his children regularly with a razor strap. Hemingway retaliated by hiding in a shed in the backyard and pointing a loaded shotgun at this father's head. When his father committed suicide, Hemingway felt considerable guilt, Martin speculates, even though he outwardly blamed his mother.

In his 2007 book *Strange Tribe: A Family Memoir*, grandson John Hemingway details the strain of mental illness and suicide running through the Hemingway family. In addition to Ernest and his father, sister Ursula, brother Leicester, and granddaughter Margaux all took their own lives. John Hemingway concluded, "I had my own ideas about the so-called curse, and believed it had more to do with genetics and bad luck than with voodoo. Either you had the genetic tendency for being bipolar, or you didn't."

Whatever its cause, and whether or not it was an obsession, critics are in agreement that death is a recurring theme in the writing of Hemingway and especially in the work many consider his best, *The Old Man and the Sea.* In the following viewpoints, critics discuss Ernest Hemingway's own life and death, the theme of death in *The Old Man and the Sea,* and perceptions of death in twenty-first-century America.

Chronology

1899

Ernest Miller Hemingway is born in Oak Park, Illinois, on July 21. He is the second of six children of Clarence Edmonds Hemingway, MD, and Grace Hall Hemingway.

1900

Hemingway's parents first take him to their summer cottage, Windemere, at Lake Walloon in northern Michigan. The northern Michigan landscape will be used in some of the writer's most successful short stories featuring Nick Adams.

1913–17

Hemingway attends Oak Park and River Forest High School where he writes for the school newspaper and literary magazine.

1917

Hemingway graduates high school and begins work as a cub reporter for the *Kansas City Star*.

1918

Hemingway joins an American Red Cross ambulance unit assisting the Italian army during World War I. He is severely injured by mortar fragments and heavy machine-gun fire at Fossalta at midnight on July 8. He spends months recuperating in a Milan hospital and falls in love with a nurse, Agnes von Kurowsky.

1919

Hemingway returns to the United States and receives a letter from Agnes von Kurowsky informing him she is engaged to another.

1920

Hemingway becomes a freelance writer for the *Toronto Daily Star*. He returns to Chicago to write for the monthly magazine the *Cooperative Commonwealth*. He meets Sherwood Anderson, who encourages his writing efforts.

1921

Hemingway marries Hadley Richardson on September 3 in Horton Bay, Michigan. He becomes the European correspondent for the *Toronto Daily Star*, and the Hemingways move to Paris.

1922

Hemingway becomes friends with many prominent artists and writers in Paris, including Gertrude Stein and Ezra Pound. Hadley takes a train to Lausanne, Switzerland, to join Hemingway, and in transit a thief steals her valise, which contains the manuscripts of virtually all of Hemingway's unpublished fiction.

1923

Hemingway makes his first trip to Pamplona, Spain, where he becomes fascinated by bullfighting. His son John Hadley is born in October. He publishes a limited edition volume, *Three Stories and Ten Poems*.

1924

In Our Time is published in Paris. Hemingway assists Ford Madox Ford in editing the *Transatlantic Review*, which prints "Indian Camp" and other early Hemingway stories.

1925

The US edition of *In Our Time* is published by Boni and Liveright. Hemingway travels to Spain with Hadley and a number of acquaintances for the festival of San Fermín. Several of the events and characters from this trip will be the inspiration for *The Sun Also Rises*.

1926

The Torrents of Spring, a satiric attack on Hemingway's former mentor Sherwood Anderson is published in May. *The Sun Also Rises* is published in October and is a critical success.

1927

Hemingway divorces Hadley and marries Pauline Pfeiffer, a wealthy American working as a fashion writer in Paris. His short story collection *Men Without Women* is published.

1928

Hemingway moves with Pauline to Key West, Florida, where their son Patrick is born. Hemingway's father commits suicide.

1929

A Farewell to Arms is published and is a commercial success.

1931

Son Gregory Hancock is born to Hemingway and Pauline.

1932

Death in the Afternoon, a lengthy study of bullfighting, is published.

1933

Winner Take Nothing, a collection of short stories, is published. Hemingway goes on safari to Africa.

1935

Green Hills of Africa, based on Hemingway's experiences in Africa, is published.

1936–1937

Hemingway travels to Spain to cover the Spanish Civil War for the North American Newspaper Alliance. He works on a propaganda film, *The Spanish Earth*. *To Have and Have Not* is published. Hemingway begins an affair with Martha Gellhorn, a journalist and writer.

1938

The Fifth Column and the First Forty-Nine Stories is published.

1939

Hemingway travels to Cuba to begin writing a novel on the Spanish Civil War. Martha Gellhorn follows him.

1940

For Whom the Bell Tolls, based on Hemingway's experiences in the Spanish Civil War, is published and dedicated to Gellhorn. Pauline divorces Hemingway, and he marries Martha Gellhorn in Sun Valley, Idaho, and moves with her to Havana, Cuba.

1942

Men at War, a collection of war stories, is published. Hemingway proposes to the American embassy that he set up a private counterintelligence agency, and he outfits his boat, *Pilar*, to hunt German submarines in the Caribbean at the beginning of World War II.

1942–1945

Hemingway covers World War II in Europe as a newspaper and magazine correspondent. He observes D-day—the Normandy invasion of June 6, 1944, by the Allies—firsthand and attaches himself to the Twenty-second Regiment, Fourth Infantry Division, for operations leading to the liberation of Paris. He begins an affair with Mary Welsh, an American journalist.

1944

Hemingway divorces Martha Gellhorn and marries Mary Welsh in Havana.

1947

Hemingway receives the Bronze Star for war service during 1944.

1950

Across the River and into the Trees is published and critically savaged.

1952

The Old Man and the Sea is published.

1953

Hemingway receives the Pulitzer Prize for *The Old Man and the Sea*. He returns to Africa with Mary for a safari.

1954

In January, Hemingway is severely injured in two successive plane crashes in Africa and is erroneously reported dead. He is awarded the Nobel Prize in Literature.

1960

Hemingway moves with Mary to Ketchum, Idaho. He suffers a nervous breakdown and enters the Mayo Clinic, where he undergoes electroshock therapy treatments.

1961

Beset by declining health, depression, and paranoia, early on the morning of July 2 Hemingway commits suicide by a gunshot to the head; he is buried in Sun Valley, Idaho.

1964

A Moveable Feast, a memoir of Hemingway's experiences in Paris in the 1920s, is published.

1970

Islands in the Stream, a semiautobiographical novel, is published.

1972

The Nick Adams Stories, a collection including some previously unpublished stories and fragments, is published.

1980

The Ernest Hemingway Collection at the John F. Kennedy Presidential Library in Boston is opened to the public.

1981

Ernest Hemingway: Selected Letters, 1917–1961, edited by Carlos Baker, is published.

1986

The Garden of Eden, a heavily edited and compressed version of Hemingway's last unfinished manuscript about love affairs between two women and one man, is published.

Background on Ernest Hemingway

The Life of Ernest Hemingway

John C. Unrue

John C. Unrue is a professor specializing in twentieth-century American literature at the University of Nevada, Las Vegas.

Throughout his life, Ernest Hemingway was fascinated by violence, death, and suicide, writes Unrue in the following viewpoint. Stories that he wrote for his high school literary magazine have death as a theme, as do the early Nick Adams stories that were collected in In Our Time, *Unrue reports. In one of his later works,* The Old Man and the Sea, *the travails of the old fisherman Santiago are meant to reflect Hemingway's struggle to continue writing while besieged by poor health, injuries, and depression, the critic explains.*

By the time he was thirty years old, Ernest Hemingway was considered a stylistic master, and his stories and novels influenced a generation of writers. From the beginning of his writing career Hemingway created a persona and legend, causing many to conclude that Ernest Hemingway's greatest character was himself. Yet, he was not one character but several, underscoring [novelist] F. Scott Fitzgerald's observation about the difficulty of writing a good biography of a novelist because "he is too many people if he is any good."

Hemingway Was Highly Competitive

Hemingway translated his life into art in a series of stages during which he moved himself into his fictional world, first in his letters and his newspaper articles, becoming the character later developed in the conventional and disciplined stages of his composition. It was a process by which he became a part of a fiction from which he did not always extricate him-

From *EBK: Dictionary of Literary Biography* Vol 330. © 2007 Cengage Learning.

self. Consequently, he is so closely bound to his fictional characters that it is difficult to separate him from them.

Hemingway was fiercely competitive. As a sportsman he wanted to be the best fisherman or hunter, but his greatest goal was to be the best writer. He told his father in 1925 that in his writing he wanted "to get the feeling of actual life across—not just to depict life or criticize it—but to actually make it alive." Hemingway was a complicated man, proving himself capable of brutality and betrayal as well as kindness and compassion. When he published *The Old Man and the Sea* (1952), he said that he "tried to make a real old man, a real boy, a real sea and real sharks," and that if he "made them true enough they would mean many things." He was speaking not only of his novella, but also of his life and art.

Ernest Miller Hemingway was born in Oak Park, Illinois, an affluent and conservative suburb of Chicago, on 21 July 1899. He was the second of six children and the first son of Clarence Edmonds Hemingway, a physician, and Grace Hall Hemingway. In childhood and adolescence Hemingway spent summers with his family at Windemere, their house at Lake Walloon in northern Michigan in the area of Petoskey. His hunting and fishing adventures and his contact with the Ojibway Indians, as well as his observations of the troubled relationship between his parents, became the material for stories such as "Indian Camp" (1925), "Ten Indians" (1927), "The Doctor and the Doctor's Wife" (1924), "The End of Something" (1925), "The Three-Day Blow" (1925), and "Fathers and Sons" (1933), all featuring Nick Adams, a recurrent Hemingway autobiographical protagonist.

Hemingway also derived from his parents positive and enduring values that shaped his career and guided his conduct. His mother introduced him to the arts and made books available. His father instilled in him a respect for and knowledge of nature.

Despite its religious fundamentalism, political conservatism, and adherence to what it saw as moral certainties, the village of Oak Park was progressive: It had a good library and a high school that provided Hemingway with a sound education, especially in composition, language, literature, and history. He read Geoffrey Chaucer, William Shakespeare, John Milton, Alexander Pope, and Matthew Arnold, and he gained valuable experience writing for the school newspaper, the *Trapeze*, and its literary magazine, *Tabula*, to which he contributed three stories during his junior year that reveal his early interest in violent death and suicide. Hemingway's competitive spirit drove him to box, play football, and run track, but he was never an outstanding athlete.

The Young Hemingway Becomes a Journalist

Between November 1916 and May 1917 Hemingway wrote twenty-four articles for the *Trapeze*. Although the quality of his work was unexceptional, his experience helped prepare him for his first job following high school, as a cub reporter with the *Kansas City Star*, considered one of the best newspapers in America. In addition to having the advice of first-rate journalistic professionals, Hemingway had to make his writing comply with the 110 rules of the *Kansas City Star* style sheet, requiring him to avoid adjectives and to use short sentences, brief paragraphs, vigorous English, and fresh phrases. Later, Hemingway remarked that these rules, which influenced his style as a fiction writer, were the best he had ever learned.

Determined to get to Europe and participate in World War I, which the United States had entered in the spring of 1917, Hemingway left the *Kansas City Star* at the end of April 1918 and joined an American Red Cross ambulance unit that assisted the Italian army. On 8 July at Fossalta he was hit by shrapnel from an Austrian trench mortar and suffered severe leg wounds. He was sent to an American Red Cross hospital in Milan.

When Hemingway arrived home in January 1919, he exaggerated his war service, creating a heroic persona for himself that he embellished throughout most of his life. He pursued a writing career ever more diligently, imitating Rudyard Kipling, O. Henry [the pen name of William Sydney Porter], and Ring Lardner, optimistic that he could follow a formula that would enable him to sell his stories to the *Saturday Evening Post* and other mass-market magazines. But he had yet to find his own narrative voice or his own material, and his work, predictably amateurish, was rejected.

Hemingway left home in January 1920 for Toronto, where he became a freelancer for the *Toronto Star*. He returned to Chicago in May and worked for the *Cooperative Commonwealth*, a monthly magazine. He met and became engaged to twenty-eight-year-old Hadley Richardson, whom he married on 3 September 1921 in Horton Bay, Michigan. In Chicago he also met Sherwood Anderson, whose *Winesburg, Ohio* (1919) had gained wide acclaim. Anderson befriended Hemingway, encouraged his writing efforts, and convinced him that Paris was the place for a serious writer. Supported by Hadley Hemingway's trust fund, which yielded approximately $3,000 annually, Hemingway and his wife left for Paris at the end of the year. He carried letters of introduction from Anderson to Gertrude Stein, Sylvia Beach (owner of the bookstore and lending library Shakespeare and Company), and Ezra Pound. . . .

In August 1923 [Robert] McAlmon published Hemingway's first book, *Three Stories and Ten Poems*. Although the poems in the volume merited little acclaim, the stories—"My Old Man," an initiation story about horse racing with a narrative voice bearing a resemblance to that in Anderson's "I Want to Know Why"; "Up in Michigan," a seduction story Stein thought too sexually explicit to be publishable; and "Out of Season," about tension and conflict in a marriage during a fishing trip in Italy—received praise. Hemingway and his wife left Paris for Toronto, where he was on salary as a full-time reporter with the *Toronto Star*. There they awaited the birth of their child and news of Hemingway's second book, *In Our Time*, which William Bird published in 1924. John Hadley Nicanor (Bumby) Hemingway was born in Toronto on 10 October 1923. . . .

In Our Time Is a Modest Success

In late April 1925, in the Dingo Bar in Montparnasse, Hemingway met Fitzgerald. Despite Fitzgerald's being the established and successful writer, with two collections of short stories and three novels, including *The Great Gatsby* (1925), while Hemingway had published two slim volumes totaling eighty-eight pages and 470 copies, Fitzgerald was in awe of Hemingway, impressed by his talent and intimidated by him. Their meeting was the beginning of one of the most complex friendships in American literary history.

In March, Hemingway had signed a contract with Boni and Liveright for his first trade publication, a collection of stories called *In Our Time*. The new book consisted of fifteen stories and reprinted vignettes from *In Our Time*; it included seven Nick Adams stories, showing Nick as a child and young man experiencing initiation as he confronts death, insanity, loss, disillusionment, consequences of matrimony and fatherhood, and in the best story, "Big Two-Hearted River," healing and revitalization on a trout stream. *In Our Time* was published on 5 October 1925. Although the collection includes some excellent stories and reveals Hemingway's talent, it did not sell well.

Nevertheless, reviewers praised *In Our Time* and saw in Hemingway's vignettes and stories what critic Edmund Wilson had called earlier in a review for *Dial* (October 1924) of *Three Stories and Ten Poems* and *In Our Time* "a distinctively American development in prose" that was "strikingly original.". . .

In July 1925 Hemingway and Hadley Hemingway [traveled] to the fiesta of San Fermín with humorist Donald Ogden Stewart; Bill Smith, Hemingway's old fishing friend from northern Michigan; novelist Harold Loeb; Lady Duff Twysden, an alcoholic Englishwoman and Montparnasse fixture; and her alcoholic Scottish fiancé, Pat Guthrie. Hemingway experienced the excitement of the fiesta and observed the tension, jealousy, resentment, and bad behavior in the group. When the fiesta concluded, Hemingway began writing a new novel [*The Sun Also Rises*]. Paris, Spain, his friends, the fiesta, and the brilliant young bullfighter Niño de la Palma provided the material. He finished the first draft on 21 September. . . .

Hemingway's Reputation Grows

The Hemingways returned to Pamplona in July, taking along other friends, including Pauline Pfeiffer, a wealthy American who worked for the Paris edition of *Vogue* and who had accompanied the Hemingways on skiing trips to Austria. By the end of the festival, Hadley Hemingway knew that her husband was having an affair with Pfeiffer. The Hemingways returned to Paris and set up separate residences.

The Sun Also Rises was published on 22 October 1926. It advanced Hemingway's literary career, introducing him to an American audience and expanding his reputation beyond Paris. . . .

Hemingway's divorce from Hadley Hemingway became final in mid April 1927, and Hemingway and Pfeiffer were married in May. By March 1928 Hemingway had begun a novel inspired by some of the stories in *Men Without Women*: "In Another Country," "Now I Lay Me," and "Italy, 1927," later called "Che Ti Dice La Patria," all concerned with scenes and sentiments associated with his war experiences. The novel was *A Farewell to Arms* (1929).

Hemingway had wanted to return to the United States for several years, and he and Pauline Hemingway, who was pregnant, sailed on 17 March 1928 for Key West from France. Their son Patrick was born on 28 June 1928. Hemingway received a telegram on 6 December informing him of the death of his father. Having suffered depression for many years, Clarence Hemingway had shot himself. Following the funeral, Hemingway finished *A Farewell to Arms*. In April 1929 Hemingway and his family returned to France, where he revised the page proofs for serial publication of *A Farewell to Arms* in *Scribner's Magazine* and rewrote the ending.

A *Farewell to Arms* was published on 27 September 1929. It was praised from the outset, and the first printing of 31,050 copies sold rapidly, with additional printings in September, October, and November. By February 1930 Hemingway had earned more than $30,000 in royalties.

In *The Sun Also Rises* Hemingway had shown the effects of World War I upon the generation whose lives it touched. In his second novel he focused upon the war itself, tracing the events that took a toll on the young people who participated in it. . . .

Hemingway's Reputation Declines

On 12 November 1931 Pauline Hemingway gave birth to son Gregory, and the following month Hemingway finished *Death in the Afternoon*. It was published on 23 September 1932. Although the book revealed Hemingway's considerable research and knowledge about bullfighting, as well as his most extensive public presentation of his writing philosophy, *Death in the Afternoon* was not embraced by Americans during the Depression. Some reviewers attacked Hemingway personally, faulting his remarks about other writers. . . .

As 1933 ended, the Hemingways went to Africa for a two-month safari. After he returned to Key West in April 1934, Hemingway began writing *Green Hills of Africa*, an experimental book in which he attempted, he said in the foreword, "to see whether the shape of a country and the pattern of a month's action can, if truly presented, compete with a work of the imagination." After appearing serially in *Scribner's Magazine*, the book was published on 25 October 1935. . . .

Most critics thought *Green Hills of Africa* a failed experiment. Leftist reviewers found Hemingway's subject inappropriate for the times and again chided him for ignoring the ills of society and for attacking political dogma and the Marxist school of writing. Many others were offended by his judgments about contemporary rival writers and thought his literary discussions self-aggrandizing and superficial. Hemingway had also attacked the critics themselves, calling them "the lice who crawl on literature."

Hemingway had begun writing a long story in February 1933 about Harry Morgan, the owner of a charter fishing boat in Key West who had become a smuggler in order to support his family during the Depression. [Editor's note: This story eventually became *To Have and Have Not*.]. . .

Hemingway became involved in the Loyalist cause in the Spanish Civil War and covered the conflict for the North American Newspaper Alliance (NANA). His personal life had also become complicated, as he had begun an affair with Martha Gellhorn, a young writer he met in Key West and who also went to Spain as a correspondent for *Collier's*. *To Have and Have Not* was published on 15 October 1937. Although a reviewer for *New Masses*, a radical magazine, thought this work better than Hemingway's previous novels, *To Have and Have Not* was generally regarded as structurally flawed and unsuccessful. Yet, it was a Hemingway book, and it sold 38,000 copies in five months. . . .

In February 1939 Hemingway went to Cuba to begin writing his much-anticipated big book on the Spanish Civil War. Following him there in April, Gellhorn rented the Finca Vigía, near Havana. By summer 1940 he had finished his novel, and

Pauline Hemingway had filed for divorce. *For Whom the Bell Tolls*, dedicated to Gellhorn, was published on 21 October 1940. . . .

The Book-of-the-Month Club selected it [*For Whom the Bell Tolls*], and Paramount Pictures paid $100,000 for movie rights. The novel sold 491,000 copies within six months of its publication. Hemingway's critical reputation, which had declined throughout the 1930s, had once again been restored, and his fame and fortune had never been greater. His divorce from Pauline Hemingway became final on 4 November 1940, and he and Gellhorn were married at Sun Valley, Idaho, on 21 November. . . .

Hemingway Covers World War II

After the publication of *For Whom the Bell Tolls*, Hemingway's literary productivity waned. At the end of 1940 he bought the Finca Vigía, and he and Gellhorn left at the beginning of the new year to cover the war in China, Gellhorn for *Collier's* and Hemingway for *PM*, a liberal New York tabloid. In his dispatches for *PM* he often appeared prophetic, predicting that the United States would be forced into war when Japan attacked American bases in the Pacific. Yet, he produced just eight articles during his Far East assignment, "only enough," he said, "to keep from being sent home." In the spring of 1942 he edited and wrote an introduction for the anthology *Men at War*, which was published in October.

With an influx of Nazi agents into Cuba and U-boats steadily sinking ships in the Caribbean, Hemingway proposed to officials at the American embassy and to the U.S. ambassador to Cuba that he set up a private counterintelligence agency. The Cuban prime minister granted him permission, and Hemingway organized a group he called the Crook Factory and outfitted his fishing boat the *Pilar* for U-boat surveillance.

Ernest Hemingway on crutches in an American Red Cross Hospital in Milan, Italy, during World War I, circa 1918. © Corbis.

During this time Hemingway's drinking increased, and his marriage deteriorated as Gellhorn spent more time away from Cuba on journalistic assignments.

At the end of October 1943 Gellhorn left Cuba again to cover the war in Europe for *Collier's*. Early in 1944 Hemingway usurped her position with the magazine, agreeing to go to

Europe for *Collier's* as their frontline correspondent, a role women were not permitted to fill. Hemingway began an affair with Mary Welsh, an American journalist in London whose marriage to Australian reporter Noel Monks also had become fragile. On D-Day, 6 June 1944, Hemingway was on a landing craft taking soldiers ashore at Omaha Beach. Biographer Michael Reynolds records that after taking German machine-gun fire trained on the boat, the lieutenant in charge put back out to sea and rejoined the attack transport *Dorothea M. Dix* that Hemingway reboarded, losing his opportunity to go ashore on D-Day (though Gellhorn did go ashore from a hospital ship on 7 June). Ten other landing craft were destroyed attempting to land. Reporting on the confusion, fear, death, and destruction, Hemingway observed, "Real war is never like paper war, nor do accounts of it read much the way it looks."

After a brief assignment as a correspondent with General George Patton's Third Army, Hemingway was assigned to the Twenty-Second Infantry Regiment, where he acted as an irregular soldier, often violating his noncombatant status. Recalling his feelings about Paris as he looked down on the city with American forces of liberation, he wrote, "I couldn't say anything more then, because I had a funny choke in my throat and I had to clean my glasses because there now, below us, gray and always beautiful, was spread the city I love best in all the world." On 25 August 1944 Hemingway entered Paris with the American and French armies.

He contributed only six articles to *Collier's* recounting his observations as a correspondent during the war. However, he wrote to Welsh from Belgium that he had material for four short stories that would provide funds while he wrote a novel. In March 1945 Hemingway returned to Cuba, and Welsh arrived shortly afterward. On 14 March 1946, their respective divorces final, Hemingway and Welsh were married in Havana.

Hemingway began an ambitious writing project in 1945, a trilogy that would encompass the land, sea, and air from the mid-1930s to the mid-1940s. He had not published any fiction for five years. He returned to a Bimini fragment he had begun before going to London in 1944 that became *Islands in the Stream* (1970). By 1946 he was also writing a novel he called *The Garden of Eden* (1986). Both novels were published posthumously. News stories and magazine articles about him increased; Hollywood bought more of his work; and the Hemingway legend grew. In 1947 he was awarded the Bronze Star for his war service during 1944. . . .

The Old Man and the Sea Is Hailed as a Masterpiece

Hemingway began writing what he considered a final section of the sea portion of his planned land, sea, and air trilogy: the story of an old Cuban fisherman who had gone eighty-four days without catching a fish and who had taken his small boat far out to sea where he hooked and fought a giant marlin for three days. After lashing the great fish to his boat, he must fight sharks that devour the fish. Hemingway clearly identified with the circumstances of the old man, who had not had a big fish for a long time, but who was "born" to fish. The conditions under which Hemingway was pursuing his art by 1951 were the most difficult he had faced. Although he was only fifty-one years old, his physical condition had deteriorated during the last decade as a result of serious head injuries, infections, and alcohol abuse, all of which exacerbated his depression.

Hemingway worked rapidly to complete *The Old Man and the Sea*, which was published in its entirety in *Life* magazine on 1 September 1952 with a printing of more than 5 million copies. The following week Scribner published it, and 50,000 copies sold out in ten days; the Book-of-the-Month Club distributed 153,000 copies. Most reviewers were effusive in their praise of the novella, saying that Hemingway had written a masterpiece and that he had returned to his true form. . . .

Hemingway Sustains Injuries in Two Plane Crashes

By the end of August the Hemingways had gone to Africa for a safari. At the conclusion of the safari, an airplane sightseeing trip on 23 January 1954 proved nearly fatal when their pilot crash-landed, leaving Mary Hemingway with broken ribs and Hemingway with back, shoulder, and arm injuries. A second plane crashed while attempting takeoff the following day, causing Hemingway serious internal injuries and a concussion. When an air search found the wreckage with no one nearby, newspapers throughout the world carried obituaries for Hemingway and his wife. Hemingway reported in "The Christmas Gift" (*Look*, 20 April and 4 May 1954) that he had been unable to resist reading his obituaries, referring to them as his "new and attractive vice" as he observed the inaccuracies of reporters. He said that a German newspaper reported that he had attempted to land one of the airplanes himself on the summit of Mount Kilimanjaro, and an Italian paper carried comments by people who called themselves his "only true and intimate friends . . . who knew the innermost contents of my heart." Nearly all obituaries, he said, "emphasized that I had sought death all my life," an observation he rejected. . . .

On 28 October 1954 it was announced that Ernest Hemingway was the winner of the Nobel Prize in Literature "for his powerful, style-forming mastery of the art of modern narration, as most recently evinced in *The Old Man and the Sea*.". . .

Hemingway Commits Suicide

Hemingway did not attend the Nobel award ceremony, excusing himself because of his recent injuries. He returned to work, writing steadily on a new African book and assisting in the filming of *The Old Man and the Sea* until illnesses, including hepatitis, put him in bed from November 1955 to January 1956. By fall Hemingway was well enough to travel to Europe, and he and Mary Hemingway stayed in Paris until January 1957. Hemingway suffered from deteriorating health during much of the trip, and by the time he sailed for the United States he had high blood pressure and an enlarged liver.

Back in Cuba, despite his poor health and constant interruptions, Hemingway returned to his work: an African book (*True at First Light*, 1999), *The Garden of Eden* (1986), and a new project, *A Moveable Feast* (1964), a memoir about Paris in the 1920s. As revolutionary activity increased in Cuba, Hemingway feared he would be a target during the overthrow of the [Fulgencio] Batista government, and he and his wife left Cuba for Ketchum, Idaho. They departed for Spain in 1959 after Hemingway agreed to write about the bullfight season for *Life* magazine. During the Spanish trip he displayed erratic behavior and hostility.

Hemingway went back to Spain in August 1960 to gather more material but returned to Ketchum in October. His depression and insomnia growing, his paranoia more obvious, and his nerves uncontrollable, he entered the Mayo Clinic in Rochester, Minnesota, at the end of November and underwent a series of electroshock therapy treatments. He was released on 22 January 1961. By March Hemingway's depression had returned, and he had to be restrained because of suicide attempts. He returned to the Mayo Clinic for additional electroshock therapy on 25 April and was released on 26 June, his psychiatrist confident of Hemingway's improvement. Back in Idaho, in the early morning of 2 July 1961, Hemingway killed himself with one of his favorite shotguns.

Five Hemingway books have been published posthumously, [*A Moveable Feast, Islands in the Stream, The Dangerous Summer, The Garden of Eden,* and *True at First Light*]. . . .

Hemingway Receives Posthumous Praise

Following Ernest Hemingway's death, authors, critics, and literary historians throughout the world spoke of his reputation and legacy. The *New York Times* carried several responses: [Lionel] Trilling said, "There is no one in the whole range of literature of the modern world who has a better claim than he to be acknowledged as a master." Van Wyck Brooks saw Hemingway as "the inventor of a style that has influenced other writers more than any other in our time." C.P. Snow said, "No novelist in the world has produced such a direct effect on other people's writing." Robert Frost observed, "His style dominated our story-telling long and short." And [William] Faulkner proclaimed, "He is not dead. Generations not yet born of young men and women who want to write will refute that word as applied to him."

Hemingway Committed Suicide When He Could No Longer Write

Robert Roper

Robert Roper writes for Obit *magazine and teaches at Johns Hopkins University.*

In the following viewpoint, Robert Roper claims that Hemingway's spectacular death threatened to eclipse his life, so that many people know him as the hard-living writer who shot himself, without being familiar with his work. Hemingway was fascinated by suicide and often talked about it, Roper states. The writer also suggests that Hemingway's family history of suicide may have played a role in the manner of his death as well as in his self-destructive life.

Now, 50 years since the death of Ernest Hemingway, the pummeling of his corpse is becoming less popular. His books remain in print. Readers continue to find him, outside the classroom as well as within. His former preeminence no longer threatens; his pumped-up maleness seems mainly sad. The 50 years since his death, by shotgun, in July 1961 have seen so much cultural outburst and evolution that the issues raised by his life now seem antique.

An Iconic Death

His death, though: That escapes change. It remains one of the iconic American deaths. He has come close to being remembered as much for his death as for his work, a terrible fate for a writer.

Hemingway left us right at the cusp, with John F. Kennedy, a Hemingway fan, fresh in the White House and symbolizing something new. February 1961, supporters of the electric new president asked the eminent novelist to contribute a handwritten tribute, and Hemingway struggled for a desperate week to write three or four sentences, weeping tears of anguish and frustration. He had just returned from the Mayo Clinic, where he had been treated for paranoid depression with many sessions of electroconvulsive therapy. Afterward his memory was gone. He was finished as a writer; for him, that meant he was finished.

A Complicated Man

Hemingway was a nasty piece of work, cruel to his wives and many of his fellow writers, not an especially good father, needy of sycophants and of pliable women to sit at his knee. He was also great company and an unforgettable presence in a room, deeply loyal to many friends, the very model of an engaged writer, fighting the biggest, hardest battles of his era. He was a premature and mature antifascist. A lover of the Spanish people, beloved of them in return, he involved himself deeply in the Spanish Civil War. Generalissimo [Francisco] Franco's victory, with the support of [Adolf] Hitler and [Benito] Mussolini, disgusted him but did not put him off political struggle.

His novel of that war, *For Whom the Bell Tolls*, tells the truth about Nazi involvement in Spain, but it's also honest about the murderousness of the Soviet agents who rushed to fight on the good side, alongside Hemingway and other right-thinking Westerners. As Hemingway pointed out, a bullet in the neck from a Soviet commissar left you just as dead as from a fascist.

About that death, though, that memorable death. Here is how it came for him:

Fashion model and actress Margaux Hemingway, granddaughter of Ernest Hemingway, committed suicide in 1996, following in the footsteps of her grandfather, Ernest, and her great-grandfather, Clarence Edmonds Hemingway. © Keystone Pictures USA / Alamy.

Hemingway's decline began at 18, with a wound suffered on the Italian front in World War I. He took over 200 pieces of shrapnel in his body and endured a massive concussion that rearranged his brain. The concussive wounds continued at an alarming rate. There were car crashes, falling skylights, fistfights, bad falls on slippery boat decks. His biographers count six major brain traumas, with others suspected. In 1954, returning from an African safari, he was in a small plane that crashed. The next day, being rushed to a hospital for treatment, he was trapped when that plane also went down, in flames. To save his wife and himself, Hemingway head-butted them out of a cabin window.

The drinking. The drinking was massive, as with [William] Faulkner and [F. Scott] Fitzgerald. By the time of his first serious wound in Italy, he knew his way around a bottle, and in his Paris years he drank with Bohemian abandon, becoming a pub-going buddy of James Joyce, a major-league drinker. Probably the most iconic bottles of wine in American literature appear in a Hemingway novel, *The Sun Also Rises*: In between bullfights and other diversions, the hero and his best friend fish for trout in the Irati River, and they stick their bottles of wine in the river to cool them down.

We need not tally every sip and guzzle. Suffice it to say that Hemingway drank seriously for 40 years, almost never missing a day. When he turned 60, he had a diseased liver, high blood pressure, bad blood cholesterol levels, type II diabetes, kidney infections, eye trouble, chronic headaches, and insomnia. Finding he lacked the old pep sometimes, he asked the doctors of his acquaintance to help him out, and they prescribed many medicines just then coming on market, such as Oreton M, a synthetic testosterone that "stimulates the development of male sexual characteristics," according to the *Physicians' Desk Reference* of 1947. The doctors also put him on Serpasil, a sedative; Doriden, a tranquilizer; Ritalin; Seconal . . . for insomnia; plus heavy daily doses of vitamins A and B for his liver.

Profoundly polluted, the writer managed to awaken at dawn every day and go to work. In his last decade, drinking for the finish line and taking all those drugs in insane combination, he wrote *Across the River and into the Trees*, *The Dangerous Summer*, *The Old Man and the Sea* (Pulitzer Prize), *A Moveable Feast*, and three long late novels, published posthumously as *Islands in the Stream*, *True at First Light*, and *The Garden of Eden*. In 1954 he won the Nobel Prize. As long as he could work he could live—wanted to live.

In 1928 his father had killed himself. Hemingway's mother sent him the revolver that his father had used—it was a Smith & Wesson his grandfather had carried in the Civil War. Hemingway was said to cherish the gun but to have been deeply disturbed by his mother's gesture.

A Family History of Suicide

He often talked about suicide. The times just after finishing a book were some of the worst for him. Even in his robust roaring 20s, world famous as an author already, he talked often about having night terrors, about feeling "contemptible," about being afraid he was losing control—"you lie all night half funny in the head and pray and pray and pray you won't go crazy." In a love letter to the woman who would become his second wife, he wrote, "I think all the time I want to die." A love letter! The inner Hemingway was agonized, was ever on the cross.

The relation of the greatness of some of his writing to his terrors and his self-loathing is no simple subject. Of his five brothers and sisters, three died by their own hand, a fourth probably also. One of his sons, Gregory, was drug addicted and deeply troubled and died in jail. One of his granddaughters, Margaux Hemingway, the actress, also was an addict and an early suicide.

Enough already! an inveterate Hemingway reader wants to say, enough of this inescapable, written-in-the-genes doom.

We do not have to admire him or forgive his excesses to think that his life was, indeed, an exercise in courage, as he often told us—just not the courage of facing down a lion, or going into combat armed with only a pencil and a reporter's pad. Courage was "grace under pressure," he said, and the head that he kept putting in the way of car windshields, bullets, and plane fuselages was terribly full of self-generated destructive forces. Why it was that way none of his biographers has ever adequately expressed. That so large and memorable a personage was so entirely without hope so much of the time awakens compassion.

With his memory mostly gone, after all that electroshock, his despair was immense. But it lifted when he convinced a staff psychiatrist at the Mayo Clinic that he was feeling better now, that it was safe to send him home. Then he was all smiles, as he hadn't been in years. At home, his shotguns awaited. Not with unseemly haste, but briskly, he made his way downstairs to the gun cabinet in his home in Ketchum, Idaho. There he put his hands on his deliverance.

The FBI Spied on Hemingway and Contributed to His Death

A.E. Hotchner

A close friend of Hemingway during the last fourteen years of the author's life, A.E. Hotchner is author of one of the best-known biographies of Hemingway, Papa Hemingway.

Fifty years after Ernest Hemingway's suicide, his good friend and biographer recalls that during the last year of the writer's life, he was suffering from extreme depression and apparent paranoia. The reasons for his depression were real—electroshock therapy had destroyed his memory and ability to write, A.E. Hotchner explains. It also turned out that his paranoia was well founded, his friend reports. In recent years, it was revealed that the Federal Bureau of Investigation (FBI) under J. Edgar Hoover was suspicious about Hemingway's Cuban connections and had him placed under surveillance. Hotchner believes that this surveillance could well have contributed to Hemingway's suicide.

Early one morning, 50 years ago today, while his wife, Mary, slept upstairs, Ernest Hemingway went into the vestibule of his Ketchum, Idaho, house, selected his favorite shotgun from the rack, inserted shells into its chambers and ended his life.

There were many differing explanations at the time: that he had terminal cancer or money problems, that it was an accident, that he'd quarreled with Mary. None were true. As his friends knew, he'd been suffering from depression and paranoia for the last year of his life.

Ernest and I were friends for 14 years. I dramatized many of his stories and novels for television specials and film, and we shared adventures in France, Italy, Cuba and Spain, where, as a pretend matador with Ernest as my manager, I participated in a Ciudad Real bullfight. Ernest's zest for life was infectious.

In 1959 Ernest had a contract with *Life* magazine to write about Spain's reigning matadors, the brothers-in-law Antonio Ordóñez and Luis Miguel Dominguín. He cabled me, urging me to join him for the tour. It was a glorious summer, and we celebrated Ernest's 60th birthday with a party that lasted two days.

But I remember it now as the last of the good times.

Hemingway Exhibits Paranoia

In May 1960, Ernest phoned me from Cuba. He was uncharacteristically perturbed that the unfinished *Life* article had reached 92,453 words. The contract was for 40,000; he was having nightmares.

A month later, he called again. He had cut only 530 words; he was exhausted and would it be an imposition to ask me to come to Cuba to help him?

I did, and over the next nine days I submitted list upon list of suggested cuts. At first he rejected them: "What I've written is Proustian [referring to the style of French writer Marcel Proust] in its cumulative effect, and if we eliminate detail we destroy that effect." But eventually he grudgingly consented to cutting 54,916 words. He was resigned, surrendering, and said he would leave it to *Life* to cut the rest.

I got on the plane back to New York knowing my friend was "bone-tired and very beat-up," but thinking he simply needed rest and would soon be his old dominating self again.

In November I went out West for our annual pheasant shoot and realized how wrong I was. When Ernest and our friend Duke MacMullen met my train at Shoshone, Idaho, for the drive to Ketchum, we did not stop at the bar opposite the station as we usually did because Ernest was anxious to get on the road. I asked why the hurry.

"The feds."

"What?"

"They tailed us all the way. Ask Duke."

"Well . . . there was a car back of us out of Hailey."

"Why are FBI agents pursuing you?" I asked.

"It's the worst hell. The goddamnedest hell. They've bugged everything. That's why we're using Duke's car. Mine's bugged. Everything's bugged. Can't use the phone. Mail intercepted."

We rode for miles in silence. As we turned into Ketchum, Ernest said quietly: "Duke, pull over. Cut your lights." He peered across the street at a bank. Two men were working inside. "What is it?" I asked.

"Auditors. The FBI's got them going over my account."

"But how do you know?"

"Why would two auditors be working in the middle of the night? Of course it's my account."

All his friends were worried: he had changed; he was depressed; he wouldn't hunt; he looked bad.

Ernest, Mary and I went to dinner the night before I left. Halfway through the meal, Ernest said we had to leave immediately. Mary asked what was wrong.

"Those two FBI agents at the bar, that's what's wrong."

Hemingway Had Nothing to Live For

The next day Mary had a private talk with me. She was terribly distraught. Ernest spent hours every day with the manuscript of his Paris sketches—published as *A Moveable Feast* after his death—trying to write but unable to do more than turn its pages. He often spoke of destroying himself and would sometimes stand at the gun rack, holding one of the guns, staring out the window.

A.E. Hotchner, left, stands beside author Ernest Hemingway. Hotchner was a close friend of Hemingway's and wrote a biography of Hemingway, Papa Hemingway, *in 1966.* © AP Photo.

On Nov. 30 he was registered under an assumed name in the psychiatric section of St. Mary's Hospital in Rochester, Minn., where, during December, he was given 11 electric shock treatments.

In January he called me from outside his room. He sounded in control, but his voice held a heartiness that didn't belong there and his delusions had not changed or diminished. His room was bugged, and the phone was tapped. He suspected that one of the interns was a fed.

During a short release, he twice attempted suicide with a gun from the vestibule rack. And on a flight to the Mayo Clinic, though heavily sedated, he tried to jump from the plane. When it stopped in Casper, Wyo., for repairs, he tried to walk into the moving propeller.

I visited him in June. He had been given a new series of shock treatments, but it was as before: the car bugged, his room bugged. I said it very gently: "Papa, why do you want to kill yourself?"

"What do you think happens to a man going on 62 when he realizes that he can never write the books and stories he promised himself? Or do any of the other things he promised himself in the good days?"

"But how can you say that? You have written a beautiful book about Paris, as beautiful as anyone can hope to write."

"The best of that I wrote before. And now I can't finish it."

I told him to relax or even retire.

"Retire?" he said. "Unlike your baseball player and your prizefighter and your matador, how does a writer retire? No one accepts that his legs are shot or the whiplash gone from his reflexes. Everywhere he goes, he hears the same damn question: what are you working on?"

I told him he never cared about those dumb questions.

Hemingway Was Right About the FBI

"What does a man care about? Staying healthy. Working good. Eating and drinking with his friends. Enjoying himself in bed. I haven't any of them. You understand, goddamn it? None of them." Then he turned on me. I was just like the others, pumping him for information and selling him out to the feds. After that day, I never saw him again.

This man, who had stood his ground against charging water buffaloes, who had flown missions over Germany, who had refused to accept the prevailing style of writing but enduring rejection and poverty, had insisted on writing in his own unique way, this man, my deepest friend, was afraid—afraid that the FBI was after him, that his body was disintegrating, that his friends had turned on him, that living was no longer an option.

Decades later, in response to a Freedom of Information petition, the FBI released its Hemingway file. It revealed that beginning in the 1940s J. Edgar Hoover had placed Ernest under surveillance because he was suspicious of Ernest's activities in Cuba. Over the following years, agents filed reports on him and tapped his phones. The surveillance continued all through his confinement at St. Mary's Hospital. It is likely that the phone outside his room was tapped after all.

In the years since, I have tried to reconcile Ernest's fear of the FBI, which I regretfully misjudged, with the reality of the FBI file. I now believe he truly sensed the surveillance, and that it substantially contributed to his anguish and his suicide.

I was in Rome the day he died.

I did not go to Ketchum for the funeral. Instead I went to Santa Maria sopra Minerva, one of his favorite churches, and said goodbye to him there. I recalled a favorite dictum of his: Man can be destroyed, but not defeated.

The Old Man and the Sea and Death

Santiago Is at Peace Because He Understands His Connection to Humanity

Richard B. Hovey

Richard B. Hovey was a professor of English at the University of Maryland at College Park and the author or contributor to numerous books, including Hemingway: The Inward Terrain.

Santiago is an unusual Hemingway hero because he is essentially at peace with himself and the world, suggests Richard B. Hovey in the following viewpoint. Hovey goes on to explain that Santiago is the Hemingway hero most closely in tune with nature. Although Santiago meditates on the struggle between life and death during his epic battle with the marlin and sharks, in his musings he accepts his role in the balance of nature, the critic contends. The old fisherman understands the law of kill and be killed—he just didn't think the struggle would be so difficult, Hovey concludes.

In 1950 [Ernest] Hemingway embarrassed us with his worst book, *Across the River and into the Trees.* Two years later, he astonished us with *The Old Man and the Sea.* Somehow he had regained control of his art. Out of his inner conflicts as a man and artist he had achieved a harmony which makes this, in a classical sense, the sweetest and most serene of his works. Whatever its shortcomings, *The Old Man and the Sea* will stand in relation to the body of Hemingway's writings as *Billy Budd* does to [Herman] Melville's.

Hemingway's Subject Is the Nature of Man

Both authors explored the power of blackness. In each of these books they tried, near the end of their careers, to say *yea* to life. Whether or not Hemingway wins us over to an affir-

From *Short Story Criticism*, 0E. © 2000 Cengage Learning.

mation, we have here his most philosophical story. A tale of adventure, *The Old Man and the Sea* is also one of those fictions where the thought and the action are one. We might label it Hemingway's summa [work that sums up a life's work]— the summa of his lifelong preoccupation with the questions of evil, of heroism, and of love. His subject is man in nature and the nature of man. For all his affectionate description of nature's beauties, Hemingway never lets us forget the Darwinian [referring to the teachings of evolution by Charles Darwin] struggle going on beneath and above the Gulf waters. Against such naturalism, we are made continually aware of Santiago's fellow feelings for nature's creatures. His tenderness toward them reminds us of Francis of Assisi.

This dualism is embodied in the old Cuban fisherman. Santiago is unique among Hemingway heroes. By chance, not by choice, is his manhood challenged. He is not on a battlefield or in a bullring or meeting a lion's charge or otherwise facing the likelihood of sudden death—nor is he recovering from a wound. With a long streak of bad luck behind him, Santiago at the start is more like, say, a farmer who has had a series of poor harvests. His predicament is that of average humanity in its day-to-day effort to keep going. That is why he is more broadly representative of the human race than any other Hemingway character. In fact, his is precisely the sort of figure so far absent from Hemingway's fiction.

Santiago Is at Peace with the World

Of course Santiago demonstrates and lives the "code." But, though sometimes his strife becomes violent and desperate, he is not a desperate man and is without inward violence. He is more or less at peace with himself, and he is not at war with his world. His physical heroism is incidental to the routine need of earning his daily bread. Since what he endures is not edged by masochism, it never exacerbates our nerves. Naturally we feel with Santiago his hurts; but these occupy us, as they do him, more as practical impediments than badges of heroism.

Besides, of all the Hemingway protagonists, Santiago is closest to nature—feels himself a part of nature; he even believes he has hands and feet and a heart like [that of] the big turtles. At first we think of him as a simple man, a primitive. Under such a guise, however, we have a wonderfully sensitive and contemplative person. He by no means lives—in [classical Greek philosopher's] Socratic phrase—the unexamined life. He asks the eternal questions. We can easily imagine another old fisherman undergoing Santiago's ordeal with equal physical courage and yet never having the surface of his mind or conscience troubled. On those vast blue waters, Santiago is a speck of intense human consciousness. It is because he is so aware of himself and the world around him that he calls himself, more than once, "a strange old man." This is also why the boy, Manolin, tells him, "There are many good fisherman and some great ones. But there is only you." For the essence of Santiago's test is spiritual—a question of what shall a man believe. And the essential courage he demonstrates is moral—even intellectual—courage in his ceaseless self-examination.

Love and Death Are Intertwined

What comes of his self-examination, this inquiry into the nature of man, these questions put to the universe? On the Gulf waters, Santiago meditates on the drama of love against hate and of life against death which nature eternally stages for us. He thinks the little terns have a harder life than we human beings have: "Why did they make birds so delicate and fine as those sea swallows when the ocean can be so cruel?" But for Santiago the ocean is not necessarily an antagonist. He regards it "as feminine and as something that gave or withheld great favours, and if she did wild or wicked things, it was because she could not help them." When he gets farther out, he sees a man-of-war bird circling and diving, and then "flying fish spurt out of the water and sail desperately over the surface." Santiago knows that the fish fly so desperately because dolphins are chasing them while the bird is trying to catch one of them: "It is a big school of dolphin, he thought. They are widespread and the flying fish have little chance. The bird has no chance. The flying fish are too big for him and they go too fast." Though always Santiago feels involved in affectionate kinship with creatures who must prey on one another, he knows he in his turn must prey on them. These musings—the torment of their ambivalence and of their ambiguities—are of course dramatized in his struggle with the big fish. . . .

Everywhere are proofs of Eros [creation] and its antagonist death. While drawn through an island of Sargasso weed "that heaved and swung in the light sea as though the ocean were making love with something under a yellow blanket," Santiago catches and kills a beautiful dolphin which flaps "wildly in the air . . . in the acrobatics of its fear. . . ." As the duel continues through the second night, his conscience puzzles over these killings: "Then he was sorry for the great fish that had nothing to eat and his determination to kill him never relaxed in his sorrow for him." How many people will this marlin feed? he wonders. But, "There is no one worthy of eating him from the manner of his behavior and his great dignity." Of these painful mysteries he can only tell himself: "But it is good that we do not have to try to kill the sun or the moon or the stars. It is enough to live on the sea and kill our true brothers." When the old man manages to doze a little, though, he does not dream of killing; he dreams of a vast school of porpoises in their mating time and he dreams of lions as harmlessly playful as happy lambs.

The Difference Between Destruction and Defeat

By sunrise of the third day, the marlin begins to circle. Santiago, though faint and dizzy, is able to pull the tiring marlin closer to his boat. Yet again the fish swims away:

You are killing me, fish, the old man thought. But you have a right to. Never have I seen a greater, or more beautiful, or a calmer or more noble thing than you, brother. Come on and kill me. I do not care who kills who.

So in this mortal battle, fish and man become one, killer and killed become one. Still, there is nothing here like the sickly caressing of the dead kudu in *Green Hills of Africa*. Rather, the context might remind us of [Ralph Waldo] Emerson's paradoxes in the poem "Brahma":

If the red slayer think he slays,

Or if the slain think he is slain,

They know not well the subtle ways

I keep and pass, and turn again.

At last comes the chance, and Santiago drives the harpoon into the marlin's heart: "'I am a tired old man. But I have killed the fish which is my brother....'"

When he lashes the great carcase to his skiff and begins the long trip back to land, Santiago believes his lacerated hands will heal quickly in the salt water:

The dark water of the true gulf is the greatest healer that there is. . . . With his mouth shut and his tail straight up we sail like brothers. Then his head started to become a little unclear and he thought, is he bringing me in or am I bringing him in?

An hour later the first shark hits: a giant Mako, "and everything about him was beautiful except his jaws...." Santiago succeeds in putting his harpoon into the Mako's brain. This time he is pure killer, kills with hate; and we infer both the masochism and the sadism of this killing: "He hit it with his blood mushed hands driving a good harpoon with all his strength. He hit it without hope but with resolution and complete malignancy." But the shark has already succeeded in mutilating the marlin; and it is as if Santiago himself has been hit. He fights his despair: "'But man is not made for defeat,' he said. 'A man can be destroyed but not defeated.'"

Unquestionably, this is the explicit moral of *The Old Man and the Sea*. And yet Santiago has an afterthought: "I am sorry that I killed the fish, though." He says he has no "understanding" of sin, yet he wrestles with his conscience:

> Perhaps it was a sin to kill the fish. I suppose it was even though I did it to keep me alive and feed many people. But then everything is a sin. Do not think about sin. It is much too late for that and there are people who are paid to do it. Let them think about it. You were born to be a fisherman as the fish was born to be a fish. San Pedro was a fisherman as was the father of the great [baseball player Joe] DiMaggio.

Such reflections bring no comfort:

> You did not kill the fish only to keep alive and to sell for food, he thought. You killed him for pride and because you are a fisherman. You loved him when he was alive and you loved him after. If you love him, it is not a sin to kill him. Or is it more?

> "You think too much, old man," he said aloud.

> But you enjoyed killing the *dentuso* [shark], he thought. He lives on the live fish as you do. He is not a scavenger nor just a moving appetite as some sharks are. He is beautiful and noble and knows no fear of anything.

> "I killed him in self-defense," the old man said aloud. "And I killed him well."

> Besides, he thought, everything kills everything else in some way. Fishing kills me exactly as it keeps me alive.

Then Santiago undercuts these gloomy musings by reminding himself that it is the love of Manolin which also

Author Ernest Hemingway stalks an elephant while on a big game hunt in September 1952 in Kenya. © Earl Theisen/Archive Photos/Getty Images.

keeps him alive. Here is no mystique of death. This Hemingway hero is no self-destroyer, not death obsessed. Santiago is philosophical, is thinking about death, not morbidly agonizing over it. . . .

Santiago Is Aware of the Kill-and-Be-Killed Law

Whether Santiago can be labelled a tragic hero in anything like an [ancient Greek philosopher] Aristotelian sense is a problem which arises when we speculate on the question the protagonist puts to himself: What defeated him? Does he err through being too much the individualist, going it alone, and going out too far? If so, that is because circumstances force him to. Santiago declines the boy's offer to accompany him because he is considerate and not selfish. Since Manolin is a poor boy who is now with a lucky boat, it would not have been sensible for him to throw in his lot with a fisherman who has been making no catches. Santiago takes the risk of going far beyond the usual fishing grounds because, with such poor luck for eighty-four days, he must try something radical.

He sets out with no prideful individualism. The pride he takes in his strength and skill is a part of his healthy self-love, the normal pride any worker should take in worthwhile work. When the boy insists that Santiago is unique among the fishermen—"'there is only you'"—he is happy with the compliment; but he adds: "'I hope no fish will come along so great that he will prove us wrong.'" When Manolin expresses his faith in him: "'I may not be as strong as I think,' the old man said. 'But I know many tricks and I have resolution.'" He is never one who overestimates himself. Had he not correctly estimated his physical and moral strength, his venture would have been foolhardy at the outset.

Naturally in the heat of battle with the great marlin, Santiago's pride does grow. This, however, is scarcely the sort of overweening pride which drives a man out of his place in the order of things, angering the gods and bringing on their punishment. Of the moment of the actual kill, Hemingway writes: "He took all his pain and what was left of his strength and his long gone pride and he put it against the fish's agony. . . ." Santiago feels no pride at the kill: "The old man felt faint and sick and he could not see well." Afterwards he is simply sorrowful: "I am a tired old man. But I have killed this fish which is my brother. . . ." He is not punished for pride. He suffers for two reasons: the lucky accident of hooking so extraordinary a fish; the consequences of going far out which increased the likelihood of sharks getting his trophy. The coming of bad luck with the sharks does not surprise Santiago. When he looks for a reason why he has lost, he can only say, "'I went out too far.'" That is all he knows. That is all we know. With good luck, he got his fish; with better luck he might have escaped the sharks. But he was not rebelliously challenging the nature of things. Nor does he glimpse, as the heroes of classic tragedy sometimes do, some fresh awareness of his own nature, some new insight into the workings of the universe. From the beginning, he knew himself well enough and he knew the law of kill and be killed. His only lesson is that defeat is easier than he thought it might be.

The Old Man and the Sea Is a Tender Book

This book, however, is not nihilistic nor deeply pessimistic. More than any of Hemingway's earlier works it reconciles us to our human condition. Compare it, for instance, with *A Farewell to Arms*, and we see the distance Hemingway has travelled. Lt. Henry thinks that the world "kills the very good and the very gentle and the very brave. If you are none of these things you can be sure it will kill you too but there will be no special hurry." Santiago is very good, very gentle, very brave; but he has not been killed in a hurry. At the end he is asleep, dreaming of his happy lions, while the boy who loves him watches at his side. From the outset Santiago understands instinctively what Harry Morgan glimpsed only in his death agony: "No matter how a man alone ain't got no bloody f---ing chance." Of Robert Jordan's solidarity with humanity [in *For Whom the Bell Tolls*] certain questions nag us: for all his professor's intellect, Jordan's cause is verbalized in clichés, never quite dramatized in his experience. By contrast, the love which binds Santiago to nature and his fellow human beings is always realized. He is lonely but not isolated. He has not rejected the world nor cut himself off from his fellows.

Of the love realized in *The Old Man and the Sea*, Hemingway makes plain enough its values. In effect, he tells us that there are persons like Santiago who have love in their hearts. He sees evidence of love also in the nonhuman world. Alive as the hero is to the love in himself and in nature, he is equally alive to the pain, the violence, the killing which are inescapable in the natural world. Though he is tormented that he, too, must bring pain and death, at least Santiago knows that the love he feels is somehow allied with the love in nature. Before the paradox of this fact, Hemingway does not flinch. It is writ large in every ambiguity, in every ambivalence, of Santiago's adventure with the marlin. As a killer, Santiago is a breed apart from all the earlier Hemingway killers. As to that pride in giving the godlike gift of death, Santiago is a world's distance away from the matadors of *Death in the Afternoon*.

More than anywhere else in his writings, Hemingway has succeeded here in expressing tenderness—without the tight lips, or the oblique implications. If he embarrassed us with love's tenderness in *Across the River and into the Trees*, that is because in Colonel Cantwell, Hemingway was too much entangled subjectively. By contrast, there is no such fumbling in the characterization of Santiago, and no false notes in his story—despite the aging Hemingway being something of a Santiago himself. He too had fished for big ones in the Gulf Stream; and sharks had eaten away one of his own great catches. But he has never slipped into exploiting the legend of Papa the great sportsman.

Nevertheless, it is Hemingway's deeply personal involvement which gives this novelette a convincingness lacking—except in a few of the stories—in all his other writings since *Winner Take Nothing*. Here at last he has found—and found a way to realize in fiction—the warmth and tenderness and intimacy of love. A love which affords a reprieve against violence, pain, and death gives this story its poignancy. Part of Hemingway's success comes from his attitude toward his subject. It required the disciplined love of the artist to create a hero who, without too much self-love or self-hate, can still interest us.

Hemingway Believes Heroic Man Can Transcend Pain and Tragedy

Leo Gurko

Leo Gurko was a professor of English and the author of numerous works of literary criticism and biography, including Ernest Hemingway and the Pursuit of Heroism.

The Old Man and the Sea *is unique among Ernest Hemingway's novels for its more optimistic tone, maintains Leo Gurko in the following viewpoint. In this later work, the world is still filled with violence and death, but the individual can live a heroic life, Gurko writes. Santiago is a much more purposive hero than earlier Hemingway protagonists and more strongly connected to the natural world, the critic explains.*

Most of [Ernest] Hemingway's novels emphasize what men cannot do, and define the world's limitations, cruelties, or built-in evil. *The Old Man and the Sea* is remarkable for its stress on what men can do and on the world as an arena where heroic deeds are possible. The universe inhabited by Santiago, the old Cuban fisherman, is not free of tragedy and pain but these are transcended, and the affirming tone is in sharp contrast with the pessimism permeating such books as *The Sun Also Rises* and *A Farewell to Arms*.

There Is Harmony in Nature

One aspect of this universe, familiar from the earlier works, is its changelessness. The round of nature—which includes human nature—is not only eternal but eternally the same. The

Leo Gurko, "The Old Man and the Sea," *College English*, vol. 17, no. 1, October 1955, pp. 11–15.

sun not only rises, it rises always, and sets and rises again without change of rhythm. The relationship of nature to man proceeds through basic patterns that never vary. Therefore, despite the fact that a story by Hemingway is always full of action, the action takes place inside a world that is fundamentally static.

Moreover, its processes are purely secular in character: Hemingway's figures are often religious but their religion is peripheral rather than central to their lives. In *The Old Man and the Sea*, Santiago, the principal figure, is a primitive Cuban, at once religious and superstitious. Yet neither his religion nor his superstitious beliefs are relevant to his tragic experience with the great marlin; they do not create it or in any way control its meaning. The fisherman himself, knowing what it is all about, relies on his own resources and not on God (in whom he devoutly believes, just as Jake Barnes [protagonist of *The Sun Also Rises*], while calling himself a bad Catholic, is also a devout believer). If he succeeds in catching the fish, he "will say ten Our Fathers and ten Hail Marys . . . and make a pilgrimage to the Virgen de Cobre," but these are rituals that come after the event and have no significant relationship with it.

In this universe, changeless and bare of divinity, everyone has his fixed role to play. Santiago's role is to pursue the great marlin, "That which I was born for," he reflects; the marlin is to live in the deepest parts of the sea and escape the pursuit of man. The two of them struggle with each other to the death, but without animosity or hatred. On the contrary, the old man feels a deep affection and admiration for the fish. He admires its great strength as it pulls his skiff out to sea, and becomes conscious of its nobility as the two grow closer and closer together, in spirit as well as space, during their long interlude on the Gulf Stream. In the final struggle between them, his hands bleeding, his body racked with fatigue and pain, the old man reflects in his exhaustion:

> You are killing me, fish. . . . But you have a right to. Never have I seen a greater, or more beautiful, or a calmer or a more noble thing than you, brother. Come on and kill me. I do not care who kills who.

On the homeward journey, with the marlin tied to the boat and already under attack from sharks, Santiago establishes his final relationship with the fish, that great phenomenon of nature:

> You did not kill the fish only to keep alive and to sell for food, he thought. You killed him for pride and because you are a fisherman. You loved him when he was alive and you loved him after. If you love him, it is not a sin to kill him.

A sense of brotherhood and love, in a world in which everyone is killing or being killed, binds together the creatures of nature, establishes between them a unity and an emotion which transcends the destructive pattern in which they are caught. In the eternal round, each living thing, man and animal, acts out its destiny according to the drives of its species, and in the process becomes a part of the profound harmony of the natural universe. This harmony, taking into account the hard facts of pursuit, violence, and death but reaching a stage of feeling beyond them, is a primary aspect of Hemingway's view of the world. Even the sharks have their place. They are largely scavengers, but the strongest and most powerful among them, the great mako shark which makes its way out of the deep part of the sea, shares the grandeur of the marlin. Santiago kills him but feels identified with him as well:

> But you enjoyed killing the *dentuso* [shark], he thought. He lives on the live fish as you do. He is not a scavenger nor just a moving appetite as some sharks are. He is beautiful and noble and knows no fear of anything.

The Heroic Man Takes Greater Risks

Nature not only has its own harmony and integration but also its degrees of value. In *The Old Man and the Sea* this is contained in the idea of depth. The deeper the sea, the more valuable the creatures [are] living there and the more intense the experience deriving from it. On the day that he catches the great marlin, the old man goes much farther out than the other fishermen and casts bait in much deeper water. The marlin itself is a denizen of the profounder depths. Even the mako shark lives in the deep water and its speed, power, and directness are qualities associated with depth. There are, in fact, two orders in every species: the great marlins and the lesser, the great sharks and the smaller, bad-smelling, purely scavenger sharks who dwell in shallower water and attack with a sly indirectness in demeaning contrast with the bold approach of the mako. There are also two kinds of men—as there have always been in Hemingway—the greater men and the lesser, heroes and ordinary humans.

To be a hero means to dare more than other men, to expose oneself to greater dangers, and therefore more greatly to risk the possibilities of defeat and death. On the eighty-fifth day after catching his last fish, Santiago rows far beyond the customary fishing grounds; as he drops his lines into water of unplumbed depth he sees the other fishermen, looking very small, strung out in a line far inland between himself and the shore. Because he is out so far, he catches the great fish. But because the fish is so powerful, it pulls his skiff even farther out—so far from shore that they cannot get back in time to prevent the marlin being chewed to pieces by the sharks. "I shouldn't have gone out so far, fish," he said. "Neither for you nor for me. I'm sorry, fish." The greatness of the experience and the inevitability of the loss are bound up together. Nature provides us with boundless opportunities for the great experience if we have it in us to respond. The experience carries with it its heavy tragic price. No matter. It is worth it. When Santiago at last returns with the marlin still lashed to the skiff but eaten away to the skeleton, he staggers uphill to his hut groaning under the weight of the mast. He falls asleep exhausted and dreams of the African lions he had seen in his younger days at sea. The next morning the other fishermen gaze in awe at the size of the skeleton, measure it to see by how much it is record-breaking, while the reverential feeling of the boy, Manolin, for the fisherman is strongly reinforced. Everyone has somehow been uplifted by the experience. Even on the lowest, most ignorant level, it creates a sensation. The tourists in the last scene of the story mistake the marlin for a shark but they too are struck by a sense of the extraordinary.

There Is Continuity in Nature

The world not only contains the possibilities of heroic adventure and emotion to which everyone, on whatever level, can respond, but it also has continuity. Santiago is very old and has not much time left. But he has been training Manolin to pick up where he leaves off. The boy has been removed by his parents from the old man's boat because of his bad luck, but this in no way diminishes the boy's eagerness to be like Santiago. The master-pupil relationship between them suggests that the heroic impulse is part of a traditional process handed down from one generation to another, that the world is a continuous skein of possibility and affirmation. This affirming note, subdued in Hemingway's earlier fiction, is sounded here with unambiguous and unrestricted clarity.

Indeed, Santiago is the clearest representation of the hero because he is the only major character in Hemingway who has not been permanently wounded or disillusioned. His heroic side is suggested throughout. Once, in Casablanca, he defeated a huge Negro from Cienfuegos at the hand game and was referred to thereafter as *El Campéeon* [the champion]. Now in his old age, he is hero-worshipped by Manolin who wants always to fish with him, or, when he cannot, at least to help him even with his most menial chores. At sea Santiago, sharing the Cuban craze for baseball, thinks frequently of Joe DiMaggio, the greatest ballplayer of his generation, and won-

Ernest Hemingway stands with a fishing rod and a marlin, while Captain Joe Russell from Key West looks on. © Corbis.

ders whether DiMaggio, suffering from a bone spur in his heel, ever endured the pain which the marlin is now subjecting him to. And at night, when he sleeps, he dreams of lions playing on the beaches of Africa. The constant association with the king of ballplayers and the king of beasts adds to the old man's heroic proportions. He is heroic even in his bad luck. The story opens with the announcement that he has gone eighty-four days without taking a fish—ordinary men are seldom afflicted with disaster so outsized.

There Is Beauty in Nature

Heightening and intensifying these already magnified effects is the extraordinary beauty of nature which cozens and bemuses us with its sensuous intoxications. The account of the sea coming to life at dawn is one of the most moving passages in the story, supplemented later at rhapsodic intervals by the drama of the great pursuit. This comes to its visual climax with the first great jump of the marlin when, for the first time, Santiago sees the gigantic size of his prey. Hemingway pays very close attention to the rippling and fluting of the water, to wind currents, the movements of turtles, fish, and birds, the rising of sun and stars. One is filled not simply with a sense of nature's vastness, but of her enchantment. This enchantment adds an aesthetic dimension to Santiago's adventure, an adventure whose heroism invests it with moral meaning and whose invocation of comradeship and identity supply it with emotional grandeur.

Within this universe, where there is no limit to the depth of experience, learning how to function is of the greatest importance. It is not enough to have will; one must also have technique. If will is what enables one to live, technique is what enables one to live successfully. Santiago is not a journeyman fisherman, but a superb craftsman who knows his business thoroughly and always practises it with great skill. He keeps his lines straight where others allow them to drift with the current. "It is better to be lucky," he thinks. "But I would rather be exact. Then when luck comes you are ready." To be ready—with all one's professional as well as psychological resources—that is the imperative. One reason that Hemingway's stories are so crammed with technical details about fishing, hunting, bullfighting, boxing, and war—so much so that they often read like manuals on these subjects—is his belief that professional technique is the quickest and surest way of understanding the physical processes of nature, of getting into the thing itself. Men should study the world in which they are born as the most serious of all subjects; they can live in it only as they succeed in handling themselves with skill. Life is more than an endurance contest. It is also an art, with rules, rituals, and methods that, once learned, lead on to mastery.

The Hero Acts in Solitude

Furthermore, when the great trial comes, one must be alone. The pressure and the agony cannot be shared or sloughed off on others, but must be endured alone. Santiago, his hands chafed and bleeding from the pull of the marlin, his face cut, in a state of virtual prostration from his struggle, several times wishes the boy were with him to ease the strain, but it is essential that he go unaccompanied, that in the end he rely on his own resources and endure his trial unaided. At the bottom of this necessity for solitariness, there is the incurable reliance on the individual which makes Hemingway the great contemporary inheritor of the romantic tradition. The stripping down of existence to the struggle between individual man and the natural world, during the course of which he rises to the highest levels of himself, has an early echo in [John] Keats's line "Then on the shore of the wide world I stand alone. . . ." In modern fiction it is [Herman] Melville and [Joseph] Conrad who give this theme its most significant shape. The mysterious, inscrutable, dramatic nature into which their heroes plunge themselves in search of their own self-realization supplies Hemingway with the scaffolding for *The Old Man and the Sea*. Like Captain Ahab [character in Herman Melville's *Moby-Dick*], like Lord Jim [character in the Joseph Conrad book of the same name], Santiago is pitched into the dangerous ocean; for only there, and with only himself to fall back on, can he work out his destiny and come to final terms with life.

The Old Man and the Sea Affirms Life

The concept of the hero whose triumph consists of stretching his own powers to their absolute limits regardless of the physical results gives *The Old Man and the Sea* a special place among its author's works. It confronts us with a man who is not only capable of making the ultimate effort, but makes it successfully and continuously. This theme of affirmation, that had begun to be struck in *Across the River and into the Trees,* is presented here much more convincingly. Colonel Cantwell of the immediately preceding novel is forever talking about his heroism; Santiago acts his out. Cantwell reminisces on past triumphs; the old fisherman demonstrates them before our eyes. The strain of boastful exhibitionism that causes some readers to regard Hemingway as an adolescent [Lord] Byron spoiled Cantwell's story. It is almost totally absent from Santiago's.

Here we have entered a world which has to some degree recovered from the gaping wounds that made it so frightening a place in the early stories. The world which injured Jake Barnes so cruelly, pointlessly deprived Lieutenant Henry [protagonist of *A Farewell to Arms*] of his one love, destroyed Harry Morgan [protagonist of *To Have and Have Not*] at the height of his powers, and robbed Robert Jordan [protagonist of *For Whom the Bell Tolls*] of his political idealism has now begun to regain its balance. It is no longer the bleak trap within which man is doomed to struggle, suffer, and die as bravely as he can, but a meaningful, integrated structure that challenges our resources, holds forth rich emotional rewards for those who live in it daringly and boldly though continuing to exact heavy payment from them in direct proportion to how far they reach out. There is no less tragedy than before, but this has lost its bleakness and accidentality, and become purposive. It is this sense of purposiveness that makes its first appearance in Hemingway's philosophy, and sets off *The Old Man and the Sea* from his other fiction.

After the First World War the traditional hero disappeared from Western literature, to be replaced in one form or another by [Franz] Kafka's Mr. K. Hemingway's protagonists, from Nick Adams on, were hemmed in like Mr. K. by a bewildering cosmos which held them in a tight vise. The huge complicated mushrooming of politics, society, and the factory age began to smother freedom of action on the individual's part. In his own life, Hemingway tended to avoid the industrialized countries including his own and was drawn from the start to the primitive places of Spain, Africa, and Cuba. For there, the ancient struggle and harmony between man and nature still existed, and the heroic possibilities so attractive to Hemingway's temperament had freer play. At last, in the drama of Santiago, a drama entirely outside the framework of modern society and its institutions, he was able to bring these possibilities to their first full fruition, and rediscover, in however specialized a context, the hero lost in the twentieth century.

Thus *The Old Man and the Sea* is the culmination of Hemingway's long search for disengagement from the social world and total entry into the natural. This emerges in clearer focus than ever before as one of the major themes in his career both as writer and man. . . .

The movement to get out of society and its artifices is not motivated by the desire to escape but by the desire for liberation. Hemingway seeks to immerse himself totally in nature not to "evade his responsibilities" but to free his moral and emotional self. Since life in society is necessarily stunting and artificial, cowardice consists not of breaking out of it but of continuing in it. To be true to oneself makes a return to the lost world of nature categorically imperative. And that lost world, as *The Old Man and the Sea* reveals, has its own responsibilities, disciplines, moralities, and all-embracing meaning quite the equivalent of anything present in society and of much greater value because it makes possible a total response to the demands upon the self. Santiago is the first of the main figures in Hemingway who is not an American, and who is altogether free of the entanglements of modern life. It is toward the creation of such a figure that Hemingway has been moving, however obscurely, from the beginning. His ability to get inside this type of character without the fatal self-consciousness that mars so much literary "primitivism" is a measure of how far he has succeeded, in imagination at least, in freeing himself from the familiar restraints of convention.

The Old Man and the Sea Depicts a Man Coming to Terms with His Mortality

Daniel Listoe

Daniel Listoe is a senior lecturer in the English Department at the University of Wisconsin-Milwaukee.

In the later years of his writing career, Ernest Hemingway wrote about characters at the end of their lives contemplating their own deaths, Daniel Listoe asserts in the following viewpoint. In For Whom the Bell Tolls, Across the River and into the Trees, *and* The Old Man and the Sea, *each protagonist has a project he must complete in isolation before his death, Listoe declares. The critic suggests that Santiago is meant to mirror Hemingway's own situation—a heroic individual struggling alone against considerable odds to master his craft.*

The most important of Ernest Hemingway's last journeys came in the process of writing in which death could be encountered through explorations via the imagination. If the end of the man could be prepared for with the infamous demonstrations with shotgun or rifle, the artist required an advancement of craft; an intensification of his career-long study of the dead; an imaginative journey that would allow him to experience and reflect upon, through the fiction, his own death.

The Later Protagonists Prepare for Their Own Deaths

Each of the last three novels published in his lifetime demonstrates Hemingway's intense investigation of how imminent death impacts a consciousness. *For Whom the Bell Tolls, Across*

Daniel Listoe, "Writing Toward Death: The Stylistic Necessities of the Last Journeys of Ernest Hemingway," *North Dakota Quarterly*, vol. 64, no. 3, 1997, pp. 89–95. Copyright © 1997 by Daniel Listoe. All rights reserved. Reproduced by permission.

the River and into the Trees, and *The Old Man and the Sea* each offers a unique perspective on a man grappling with the knowledge of his forthcoming death.

Before "The Snows of Kilimanjaro" Hemingway wrote about death as it is observed, studied, portrayed, but not as it is anticipated. Whether in the vignettes of *In Our Time,* Catherine at the end of *A Farewell to Arms,* or the description of corpses and killing in *Death in the Afternoon,* Hemingway's initial writerly encounters with death are all exterior to the subject—they offer perceptions and reactions to others who are dead or dying. "The Snows of Kilimanjaro," however, is the sea change in Hemingway's focus. His subjects from that point forward are no longer outside death, but are forced to acknowledge and act with the certainty of their coming end.

The circumstances surrounding Robert Jordan, Richard Cantwell, and Santiago [protagonists of *For Whom the Bell Tolls, Across the River and into the Trees,* and *The Old Man and the Sea,* respectively] may be vastly different. Yet what unites them is the degree to which Hemingway, as author, seeks to inhabit their characters as those characters prepare for the death they are certain is at hand. Robert Jordan knows the danger of his mission, but also has his end forecast by Pilar. Cantwell's damaged heart and head remind him repeatedly that each bridge could be the last crossing over, that once everything has been taken care of, "there's nothing to be done." Likewise, Santiago, who is described at the outset as having "no life in his face," comes to abandon that life during the battle for his fish. Having gone "far out" into new territory while being as "exact" as he wishes, he gives himself to death saying, "Come on and kill me. I do not care who kills who."

Each Has a Project to Complete

What truly makes this trinity of death compelling is that in each case we, as readers, become witness to the compulsion of Hemingway's characters to take care of what is left for them.

In other words, each of these three protagonists must work to complete his project—whatever that may be—in the time that remains. It is as if Hemingway came to explore, again and again, the degree to which he, as a writer, could possibly complete his project as an artist. Harry in "The Snows of Kilimanjaro" is the failed writer, or rather the writer who has failed to write, and Hemingway is perhaps investigating the degree to which he—in the mid-thirties—had yet to write what was stored and waiting within his memory. The prospect of failing to accomplish what needs to be done before the coming of death appears in each of the last works. These novels can and should be read as a coherent attempt on Hemingway's part to study the psychological implications of acknowledging one's imminent death and then continuing to act in spite of death's presence.

The imperative in each novel, then, is to complete one's project before death is absolute so that in the project's completion it does not succumb to the inevitable death of the man. Santiago, Cantwell, and Jordan are each a kind of artist whose art may live and survive them. As Robert Jordan thinks before completing the blowing of the bridge: "Today is only one day in all the days that will ever be. But what will happen in all the other days that ever come can depend on what you do today."

Robert Jordan does complete his act, but then he must also reconcile himself to death through the idea that he, in some way, lives on through his actions. He accomplishes this reconciliation because of Maria and Pilar and the others who will continue on and carry his story. Through his actions they gain freedom. Wounded and slipping into death, he tells himself repeatedly to think of "them." He connects himself to Maria, saying, "Thou art all there will be of me." Hemingway merges the life acts of the man with the future in which those actions reverberate. He discovers in *For Whom the Bell Tolls* the union of a finite life and art's continuance and makes this union the basis for his portrayal of being-towards-death in the novel.

Hemingway's Heroes Face Death in Isolation

If Robert Jordan can live on through the others, Hemingway uses Cantwell and Santiago to show how a consciousness of death suffers in isolation. For example, Cantwell's project in *Across the River and into the Trees* is not one of action but of writing his life for himself. He is the self-author who tries to reclaim his life from the attendant pressures in his trade of soldiering. If Renata is the constant reminder to leave behind the sensibilities of that trade, she is also the one who listens to his stories of war and becomes audience. In Cantwell's world, she is one of the few who will listen and try to understand. But notice how often Cantwell has only himself as audience. I take the stories and reflections that comprise the bulk of the novel to be Cantwell's attempt to order and clarify, to tell the narrative of his life—a project for the sake of the self.

Santiago's attempt to catch his fish, to go "far out" in search of "one longer day" is an extension of the pattern developing in *For Whom the Bell Tolls* and *Across the River and into the Trees*. He is truly alone while attempting his project, and so we see Hemingway's intensification of having an audience of self. Hemingway grants Santiago nothing but the essential object of his art, or craft, and his own reflections and ability to think. If Santiago forges a bond with the fish then it is because they have only each other in their respective anticipations of death. When Santiago promises to battle the fish until death he utters the truth behind each of Hemingway's later characters—each is working to finish his project up until the point of his end.

Clearly the work that establishes the rest of Hemingway's writing life is "The Snows of Kilimanjaro." The portrait of

Harry is Hemingway's initiation into what he defined in *Death in the Afternoon* as complicated death. In the case of Harry, death by disease brings forth all of the self-loathing and hopeless despair occasioned by one's realization that there is no hope of completing one's project. Harry cannot look into the future and console himself as Robert Jordan does. His rotting body makes his death absolute since he cannot write nor act with resoluteness while death looms. If Hemingway was concerned for his own capacity to handle the distractions of fame and the demands of his art, then Harry can be read as that which Hemingway feared—the absolute death in which one's existence has no impact on "all the other days." . . .

There Are Parallels Between Hemingway and Santiago

The Old Man and the Sea is . . . a story of an artist whose project will remain unrecognized. . . . Santiago must . . . use his skill to keep his lines exact and thereby force the fish to circle. The fisherman is cast as artist in Hemingway's work as the language of line and craft and métier overlap and blur.

But Santiago's death . . . ends with misunderstanding and the "success" of the completed project known only to the man who dies. Santiago's isolation begins and ends the story. Through his journey, Hemingway explores the territory where one becomes fused with the project. It [is] as if Hemingway himself is uttering the words: "Come on and kill *me*. I do not care who kills who" (my emphasis). The individual who has worked to completion, who has worked exactly as one should, keeping one's lines straight throughout, is, if the word is appropriate, the victor. Death has stolen nothing from Santiago even if he, like Harry, has no trophy, for Santiago marks the fulfillment of Hemingway's attempt to render a consciousness of death and creativity in its fullest and most isolated aspects.

This journey of Santiago does, indeed, seem Hemingway's own. If there can be no confidence that the "success" will be there after death, then one must be content with the process of reflection and creation. I sense that Hemingway's frustration at not being understood, and claiming then to be in calculus, stems from the fact that his last journeys were into areas mistaken for something else. His subjects of war, lyrical remembrance, and nobility were more importantly all explorations into death's fusion with a creative consciousness. With his own time short, his own projects (those that became the posthumous works *The Garden of Eden, Islands in the Stream,* and *A Moveable Feast*) incomplete, Hemingway perhaps saw himself as one who must work alone, unwitnessed, without assurance that the kudu (the kudos) he attempted to hunt down in the mid-1930s (as described in *Green Hills of Africa*) would ever be his, that the "days to come" would ever receive the legacy he tried to offer.

Old Age Ideally Brings Humility and True Pride to Man

Stanley Cooperman

Stanley Cooperman was a poet, professor of English, and author of several works of literary criticism and biography, including two on Ernest Hemingway. Like Hemingway, Cooperman committed suicide.

The Old Man and the Sea represents Hemingway's attempt to come to terms with his own approaching old age, contends Stanley Cooperman in the following viewpoint. A man of action, Hemingway feared becoming a passive observer rather than an initiator, Cooperman explains. Although an old man, Santiago is a man of action, whose strength of spirit compensates for his weakened flesh. This romanticized version of old age—which Hemingway was never able to achieve in his own life—could have led to his decision to commit suicide, Cooperman surmises.

The preoccupation of Ernest Hemingway with individual courage, will, and endurance—the need for self-contained action, ritualized form, precision of motion (and emotion), and—perhaps most important—the fear of complex motivation and the insistence upon the absolute necessity for initiative as a definition of manhood—was seriously threatened in the years preceding and following World War II.

Hemingway's War Novels Are Unsatisfactory

The period before the war was a time of political ambiguities, a time which more than ever before represented the triumph of machines over men. And World War II itself was a difficult

Stanley Cooperman, "Hemingway and Old Age: Santiago as Priest of Time," *College English*, vol. 27, no. 3, December 1965.

matter for Hemingway to shape into art: For one thing, it was a gigantic organization in which the politician became more important than the soldier, and the mechanic became more important than both. As for the post–World War II era of "Cold War" and continuing crisis—there was simply nothing in it for Hemingway to *use*; the swamp of ideological-political-military complexities offered no solid ground on which Hemingway could stand either as a man or as a writer.

Such a war, and such complexity, could not provide for Ernest Hemingway the framework of "pure" action, the concrete and formal ritual which had always been so essential to his work. Even *For Whom the Bell Tolls* had for its setting a preliminary skirmish—the Spanish Civil War—rather than the second world conflict itself. And the novel was by no means an unmixed success; despite the fact that such Hemingway specialists as Carlos Baker see the book as a tragedy of major importance, most critics have felt that Hemingway simply could not master (in either literary or intellectual terms) the scope of material which he undertook to use. . . .

Hemingway's only other effort to produce a major novel dealing with the war against fascism—*Across the River and into the Trees*, published in 1950—gave even sharper evidence of a decline in his literary direction. In this novel there is a quality of weariness and exhaustion not simply in the book's protagonist, an aging army colonel named Richard Cantwell, but in the narrative itself. . . .

Hemingway Feared Old Age

The fact that Hemingway was attempting to deal with the problem of old age, however, was a significant development in his work, and in this sense *Across the River and into the Trees* was a milestone in his career. If the book did fail, it nevertheless served as a kind of preliminary to *The Old Man and the Sea*—a far smaller book, and a far less ambitious one, but a novel that served as a poem of reconciliation to the meaning and nature of age itself, and the manhood and courage and fierce love of creative will which redeem the flesh from its own decay.

The virtues of the Hemingway hero had always been the virtues of the young: to kill "cleanly" and risk being killed; to drink manfully, speak simply, love beautifully (and briefly), and to avoid all entanglements of either responsibility or complexity. As Harry Levin remarks: "The world that remains most alive to Hemingway is that stretch between puberty and maturity which is . . . a world of mixed apprehension and bravado before the rite of passage, the baptism of fire, the introduction to sex." Certainly it is difficult to imagine Frederic Henry [protagonist of *A Farewell to Arms*] as a fifty-year-old ex-soldier—unless, perhaps, we imagine him as Colonel Cantwell [protagonist of *Across the River and into the Trees*], "waiting" to die, and brooding upon approaching age and impotence.

So essential is the "proper" confrontation of death to the work of Ernest Hemingway that the problem of growing old seems quite irrelevant; few of his heroes are likely to grow old, and none of them will live to die in bed if they can possibly help it. As to a man outliving the days of his sexuality: This is simply too horrible to contemplate. Even the hunter in "The Snows of Kilimanjaro" dies of a wound rather than of old age, and at the time of his death, furthermore, is served by a sophisticated woman—a tribute to his strength and at least one kind of potency.

For Ernest Hemingway, far more than for most men, the spectre of age was a terrible spectre indeed; the very virtues upon which he had based his art and his life were virtues of the young. Even in his later years, Hemingway was delightfully "boyish" (or regrettably so, depending on one's point of view); the problem of age was never far from his mind nor, for that matter, from his conversation—and in this connection Lillian Ross's [1950] *New Yorker* piece on Hemingway is of particular interest. "As you get older," said Hemingway, "it is harder to have heroes, but it is sort of necessary."

The problem, of course, is to decide what sort of heroism is possible as a man gets older, and in this respect Hemingway in 1950 was still looking backward rather than forward, so that for him (as for Richard Cantwell in *Across the River and into the Trees*) old age itself was simply a matter of holding on to youthful appetites and youthful abilities as long as one could. "What I want to be when I am old is a wise old man who won't bore," he remarked to Miss Ross, while Mrs. Hemingway was saying "Papa, please get glasses fixed," and while the waiter was pouring wine. . . .

Hemingway Feared the Passivity of Old Age

From the jumble of hopes for continued youth and fears of age, however, one element emerges as perhaps the greatest fear of all—a fear that had been close to Hemingway from the crisis of his World War I experience: that is, the fear of passivity, the nightmare, a recurrent nightmare for Ernest Hemingway, in which the individual is deprived of his manhood by becoming an object rather than originator of action. Whether sitting on a park bench and "waiting for death," or growing crotchety and senile in an easy chair, or whining and complaining in a hospital bed (while the hands of stranger-women clean the body and obscenely kill the soul), the overriding fear is not loss of life ("It isn't hard to die," said Hemingway) but loss of will: the failure of manhood itself. And it was the divinity of manhood—a *mystique* defined by the sacred trinity of willed sacrifice, pride, and endurance—which Hemingway worshipped (and worried) throughout his life.

The problem, in short, was not how to avoid becoming an old man, but rather how to avoid becoming an old woman— and whether indeed an individual could be one without becoming the other. Whether Hemingway himself ever achieved a satisfactory solution to this dilemma is not for us to judge, although the circumstances of his death would indicate that he could not and would not abide a final weakening of those powers which were so intrinsic to the protagonists of his stories.

In the last decade or so of his life, at any rate, Hemingway was searching for a posture which would enable him to cope with the fact of his own age—and in a basic sense, *Across the River and into the Trees* reflected the urgency of just such a search. Hemingway's temporary but vivid solution was a change of personal role: He would dramatize what he could not avoid. "Because of his own absolute youthfulness, he regards old-growing as an utter and complete tragedy," remarked one of his friends, "and he is not going to degrade himself by maturing or anything absurd of that sort. All the same, since he has a sense of costume, he will emphasize his decline in all its hopelessness by sprouting a white beard and generally acting the part of *senex* [wise old man]. We are going to get a lot of this inverted youth from him henceforth" (quoted by Carlos Baker, *Hemingway and His Critics*).

If the early Hemingway had been an almost legendary figure of youthful and virile adventure, the older Hemingway would take up the role of Grand Old Man, the battle-scarred veteran, the aging but still indomitable combatant. Hemingway "The Champ," indeed, would become "Papa" Hemingway—the Citizen of the World still rough-edged and manfully poetic, but mellowed by experience and years, and come to full bloom as a connoisseur of life, bullfighters, women, fishing, and war.

Santiago Is a Man of Action

The resources of age rather than the powers of youth would henceforth be Hemingway's public role, and this was to provide the substance for his literary role as well. For *The Old Man and the Sea*, published in 1952, is the story not of youthful disillusion, or youthful political idealism in a framework of

Circa 1937. Novelist and journalist Ernest Hemingway at the Belchite sector during the Spanish Civil War. He was one of the first American correspondents to arrive on the scene. © London Express/Hulton Archive/Getty Images.

social affirmation, or youthful love in a world of chaos, or youthful frustration and anguish (bolstered by a code of manly non-sentiment), or not-so-youthful reminiscence relating to youth itself, but rather the story of an aged champion for whom power of will has replaced the power of flesh, and the wisdom of true pride and humility has replaced the arrogance of either simple pessimism or romantic self-sacrifice.

Humility and true pride, however, are not qualities likely to be possessed by the Crusading Idealist (such as Robert Jordan in *For Whom the Bell Tolls*), or by heroes of nostalgia (such as Colonel Cantwell in *Across the River and into the Trees*), or by protagonists of alienation—protagonists who, like Frederic Henry in *A Farewell to Arms*, refuse to play the game of life (and death) if the rules are not of their liking. The qualities of humility and pride must be forged in the smithy of a man's own soul; only when the individual neither requires nor uses external crutches—either of affirmation, negation, or nostalgia—can he achieve that power of selfhood (which for Hemingway is synonymous with manhood) that old Santiago the fisherman achieves in his open boat, alone with his pain, his endurance, his love for the noble marlin that is his opponent, his defeat, and his ultimate triumph.

This triumph, of course, is a victory in spiritual terms—for it is only in spiritual terms that a victory can ever be real. Ultimately, the only "cause" is a man's own being, his own truth; romantic love is an illusion of youth, and political or social motivation is either so complex as to be meaningless, or so corrupt as to defeat its own rhetorical purpose. Unlike Robert Jordan, Santiago does not attempt to justify his struggle in terms of externals; unlike Frederic Henry, he does not attempt to worship a sacred object—a kind of "love-goddess" for whose sake all things may be sacrificed. For Santiago, the only justification for life is living, and the only justification for death is dying: He is a fisherman and the marlin is a fish, and—joined together by a larger pattern in which each is merely a part—they fulfill their true roles.

The relationship between Santiago and the marlin is self-contained and self-meaning; not only is their struggle without hate, but—because the struggle itself is a link in that holy chain of life and death whose sole reason is its own existence—the contest becomes an act of love, almost of worship. And for Ernest Hemingway (much to the irritation of his more socially oriented or religiously orthodox critics) no act of worship could be defined in terms of group therapy. Santiago is indeed timeless; an aged monument to that power of will which finally emerges as the only means to defeat age itself, he remains a monument that stands for and by nothing but its own existence. His sainthood consists not in redeeming temporality, but rather in willing its irrelevancy.

Hemingway Explores the Theme of Isolation

The Old Man and the Sea, in short, marks a return on Hemingway's part from some attempt at social involvement to justify action, to an examination of action itself—and a hymn of praise to the sacred nature of such action, when purified by will and uncorrupted by external cause. "From the first eight words of *The Old Man and the Sea*," says Robert P. Weeks ("He was an old man who fished alone . . ."), "we are squarely confronted with a world in which man's isolation is his most insistent truth."

Human isolation: the basic *fact* of our existence, the "insistent truth" that men so often disguise by verbiage or theories, by titles or property, by all the various cosmetics and comforts offered by society, by entrenched religion, or by fleshly lusts called (or miscalled) spiritual allegiance, that they forget the isolation itself. Only in Santiago's old age, when the lusts of the flesh have cooled and the egoism and ambition of youth are no more than distant echoes, does he *act* in such a way that the act becomes its own truth: that is, he achieves divinity of manhood by means of the ritual or trinity of action consisting of willed sacrifice, pride, and endurance.

That such a ritual of manhood has only a limited relationship to brotherhood or unity in the orthodox sense is indicated by the fact that Santiago himself despises and hates those forms of life which are neither worthily beautiful nor noble; if he kills but loves the great marlin, he butchers and spits at the scavenger sharks, and his attitude toward the Portuguese man-of-war (the bladder of "beautiful poison" that floats by his boat) is one of unrelieved loathing.

There is nothing of "love thine enemy" in Santiago's attitude toward those forms of life which either through appetite or a passive show of poison (or, as in the case of the tourists at the end of the book, simple ignorance) are outside the pattern of nobility and beauty, forms of life which—because they risk nothing, do not fight purely, or feed on carrion—provide no means for a man to celebrate the sacred ritual of his own manhood.

This theme of the "initiated" versus the "outsider" is, of course, a recurrent one throughout Hemingway's work, which celebrates a brotherhood of the *worthy* and noble rather than any sort of universal love. The very definition of worthiness and nobility, moreover, depends upon whether the creature in question (bull, fish, or woman) is capable of being used, or *absorbed*, into the ritual of manhood. Since this ritual is a means (indeed, for Hemingway the only means) of establishing non-temporality through assertion of will, "nobility" becomes a matter of usefulness, while "beauty"—always in terms of the ritual itself—is defined according to its manageability.

Santiago Is a Romanticized Figure

The story of Santiago, then, clearly represents a return, or rather, a reemphasis and intensification, of the theme of isolation—the individual confronting his own destiny, and redeeming this destiny by means of a ritual of manhood which becomes its own justification. Having survived the great strength of his youth, Santiago has passed beyond all merely material ambitions and desires. There is a transcendent glow about the old man, who is himself a symbol of noble creation—that is, willed creation—with its sorrow and glory, pain and love. Divinity itself, after all, is Supreme Will ("Let there be light!" says the voice of God) rather than desire; as the embodiment of ageless will, Santiago the fisherman (who dreams of "lions") becomes an echo of the divine.

Part of the dramatic effect of *The Old Man and the Sea*, however, may be weakened by the fact that Santiago—despite his use of wisdom instead of mere strength, and of knowledge and wit instead of mere arrogance—is in many ways a romantic picture of old age itself. His very old-ness is monumental and rock-like; his endurance becomes a statement of desire rather than a human reality. For Ernest Hemingway, looking toward his own old age and attempting to construct a means of coping with it, the vision of Santiago must indeed have seemed a noble possibility. That the Santiago-solution is largely allegorical, however, is something that Hemingway could not or would not face: It is not, after all, every old age that can go out to sea in an open boat and catch giant marlin.

In the refusal (or inability) of Ernest Hemingway to see old age in any other terms but the values of pride, sacrifice, and endurance—the ritual of will he worshipped all his life (in Santiago's case forged and made harder rather than softer by old age itself), and in his insistence that the old man must be a young man grown tougher and purer, Hemingway may well have been setting up his own final tragedy.

Death Sentences: Rereading
The Old Man and the Sea

William E. Cain

William E. Cain is a professor of English at Wellesley College and the author or editor of numerous works of literary criticism. He was a coeditor of The Norton Anthology of Theory and Criticism.

Ernest Hemingway's persistent theme is that in life there is death, contends William E. Cain in the following viewpoint. The puzzle Hemingway confronts in his works is how one can create art while in the continuous process of dying, the critic maintains. The writer did not believe in life after death—the act of creating a literary work that would stand the test of time was Hemingway's measure of immortality, states Cain.

Perhaps the familiarity of *The Old Man and the Sea* has prevented us from perceiving its terrible power. Hemingway's novel has become so taken for granted that we have not appreciated how disturbing it is: for all of its intrepid dignity on the surface, it is deeply disquieting in its themes. The best known of Hemingway's books, *The Old Man and the Sea* is also the most misunderstood.

Life magazine published the entire text of *The Old Man and the Sea* in its September 1, 1952, issue and 5.3 million copies were sold in the first forty-eight hours. Scribner's first printing of 50,000 became available the next week and the book soon reached the best-seller list, where it remained for six months. The Book-of-the-Month Club chose it as a main selection with a first printing of 153,000 copies, and it was translated into nine foreign languages within the year. Soon

First published in the *Sewanee Review*, vol. 114, no. 1, Winter 2006. Copyright © 2006 by William E. Cain. Reprinted with the permission of the editor.

The Old Man and the Sea was being taught in middle schools and high schools, and it became a favorite outside the classroom as well.

Not all of Hemingway's biographers and critics admire *The Old Man and the Sea,* and some have spoken about it harshly. Jeffrey Meyers, for example, emphasizes its "radical" weaknesses, including sentimentality, self-pity, and "forced and obtrusive" Christian symbolism. "In the highly acclaimed *Old Man and the Sea,*" he states, "Hemingway either deceived himself about the profundity of his art or expressed his contempt for *Life,* Scribner's, the reading public, the critics, and religion by writing an ironic and mock-serious fable that gave them exactly what they wanted and expected." Kenneth Lynn reaches the same conclusion: "Today, there is only one question worth asking about *The Old Man.* How could a book that lapses repeatedly into lachrymose sentimentality and is relentlessly pseudo-biblical, that mixes cute talk about baseball . . . with Crucifixion symbolism of the most appalling crudity . . . have evoked such a storm of applause from highbrows and middlebrows alike—and in such overwhelming numbers?"

These are minority reports, however. Hemingway scholars usually refer to *The Old Man and the Sea* in respectful terms, describing it as Hemingway's "recovery" from the disaster of *Across the River and into the Trees,* published two years earlier, and as a noble evocation of the Hemingway code. But at present *The Old Man and the Sea* has only a marginal place in Hemingway studies. It says little about sexuality and gender— for decades these have been the dominant topics for Hemingway scholars—and hence it is briefly praised and bypassed. For most Hemingway scholars, what counts are the ambitious projects he pursued during the 1940s and 1950s, none of which he finished but which, in heavily edited and cut forms, have been published attached to his name: *A Moveable Feast*

(1964), *Islands in the Stream*, (1970), *The Dangerous Summer* (1985), *The Garden of Eden* (1986), and *True at First Light* (1999).

As revealing as these edited books are about Hemingway's personal and sexual preoccupations, in my view they do not possess the authority of the works he completed and saw through to publication in his lifetime. The climax of Hemingway's career is *The Old Man and the Sea*: this is the point at which his journey as a published writer ended. The novel lacks the range and scale of his best books of the 1920s, but it is, I believe, the work of a master, and in retrospect it strikes me as the only possible ending for his career.

I am simply proposing that we give *The Old Man and the Sea* another look and in the process allow it to display its strange brilliance. From first to last Hemingway's sentences in *The Old Man and the Sea* take surprising turns, as when he concludes the opening paragraph with a sentence about Santiago's skiff: "The sail was patched with flour sacks, and, furled, it looked like the flag of permanent defeat." "Permanent" accents the point, making it unmistakable, and thus the sentence that comes a few lines later seems a contradiction: "Everything about him was old except his eyes and they were the same color as the sea and were cheerful and undefeated." This adjustment in our response is part of Hemingway's narrative strategy: the later sentence corrects the earlier one—or, rather, it corrects our interpretation of the earlier one. The flag does not signify defeat, though to some it might be misread in that way. Hemingway is prompting us to see the difference between how something appears (and what it might mislead us to believe about a person) and who someone is.

It is frequently said that in his final books Hemingway lost contact with the shape and sound of his prose and was no longer seeing and hearing the interaction of the sentences he set down on the page. You might conclude from the novel's opening that the references first to "permanent defeat" and then to "undefeated" bear witness to the supposition that in his sentences Hemingway is not in control. But the contradiction is deliberate and dramatizes that we are inclined to make superficial judgments: we know less than we think we do. In miniature it teaches us that the reality of an experience or the essence of a person cannot be judged from surfaces. The lesson pertains to our experience and our understanding of *The Old Man and the Sea* as a whole.

This claim about Hemingway's craft can be taken further. In *The Old Man and the Sea* Hemingway is oriented critically toward his style: he reflects on its strengths and limitations and even exposes its absurdity—the arbitrariness, and yet the necessity, of choosing this word rather than that one for a sentence, and indeed the larger issue of being a writer at all. *The Old Man and the Sea* is not a recovery for Hemingway; it should not be characterized as a return to his style of the 1920s. Instead it is an advance, an effort to do something new. Hemingway seeks in this fiction to make the tragic and the comic coincide, coalescing the heroic and the laughable in his sentences. Santiago is brave and ridiculous, self-aware and out of his mind. He endures; he shows grace under pressure. He is absurd, committed to a mission and a task that matter not against the dissolution performed by time.

The storyline and plain prose of *The Old Man and the Sea* invite a rapid reading for pleasure, but the risk then is not taking the novel seriously—by which I mean with full seriousness. Hemingway's ideal audience consists of readers who pause over sentences and savor the spaces in between—the perfectly modulated sequences of notes and silences that Hemingway deploys as breathtakingly as the jazz geniuses Louis Armstrong and Miles Davis. "None of these scars were fresh," he writes of Santiago, "They were as old as erosions in a fishless desert." Hemingway gives the sense of wearing away in the sound of "old as erosions," and he implies that the scars are impossibly old, reaching backward to a desert that was once a sea. He reminds us of the span of time—that the sea in which the old man fishes will also eventually become a desert, boundless and bare.

Later, as evening falls and as the great fish that Santiago has caught continues to pull his boat, Hemingway writes:

> It was dark now as it becomes dark quickly after the sun sets in September. He lay against the worn wood of the bow and rested all that he could. The first stars were out. He did not know the name of Rigel but he saw it and knew soon they would all be out and he would have his distant friends.

> "The fish is my friend too," he said aloud. "I have never seen or heard of such a fish. But I must kill him. I am glad we do not have to try to kill the stars."

Killing the stars may sound far-fetched—some of Hemingway's critics have mocked this phrase. But there is no lapse here: such language is not far-fetched for an old fisherman tired from battle with his huge catch. This is how Santiago's mind drifts and fixes on an object of attention. The double "dark" in the first line connects Hemingway to his character—Hemingway has experienced the conditions that Santiago contends against. The vowels in "the worn wood of the bow"—the assonance of the phrase—revoke the feel of the wood's smoothness; what Santiago feels Hemingway has felt, and that is why this writer can strike the phrase that instills in us the same feeling. "The first stars were out" changes the rhythm, which is followed by Hemingway's break in point of view as he cites knowledge of a detail not known to his character and then lays down the passage of dialogue, quiet and meditative but edged with craziness.

People do talk to themselves, especially fishermen; Santiago knows he does, and Hemingway mentions this point in essays about fishing he wrote in the 1930s (e.g. "On the Blue Water," *Esquire*, April 1936). But there is more to it than that. No one else is with Santiago; he is alone at sea, occupying a jot of space amid immensity. There are no witnesses except for the reader to whom Hemingway tells the story. Those on shore, described in the final pages, see only the bare bones of the marlin; they do not know the facts and sensations of the struggle, and there is no indication that Santiago will talk about them.

Manolin, the person closest to Santiago, was not there for the contest with the marlin and the fight against the sharks either. Whatever he does hear from Santiago will be a diminished rendering of what took place. Moreover the sense of exhaustion Hemingway expresses in his character after Santiago returns to shore suggests to me that he will die very soon. Every life story ends in death, and no one knows what another person has gone through on his or her way there: the best we can achieve are approximations.

Santiago is detached from all others: nearly everyone else is a name in the newspaper or a dim recollection or a presence encountered on trips back and forth to his boat. Santiago says he loves Manolin, but it is not clear what his love amounts to. This old man would take to the sea whether Manolin existed or not. His photograph of his wife is underneath his shirt on the shelf in the corner; it made him lonely to see it, so he removed it from the wall. He does not dream about her, nor does she come to his mind when he is at sea.

Does Santiago, this figure of stark isolation, possess the grandeur that critics have attributed to him? In some measure he does, yet in truth he is just a fisherman, an old man alone, like Robert Frost's old man who can't keep a house. For many days Santiago catches no fish; he then catches a great fish only to lose it. On bad days and good days he returns to his shack, and, as Manolin is aware at the outset, this old man may not realize that some of the things he says are untrue.

There are determination and resilience in Santiago, in his devotion to his work at hand, akin to that of Hemingway rising with the sun to write and count that day's allotment of prose. This is a form of grandeur. But no exertion prevents death—the black oblivion (the other side of the white page of an author's book) into which all subsides. Day after day this knowledge pressed on Hemingway, and he is working through it in his depiction of Santiago. No writer was more severely driven by the imperative to work, nor was any writer more cut to the quick by the hopelessness of work shadowed by extinction.

In *The Old Man and the Sea* Hemingway recounts Santiago's story to express the majesty and the pointlessness of human effort. It is not that he is using Santiago as an analogy for himself as a writer. He is saying he and Santiago are the same. It is simple: one fishes, one writes, both die. This is not sentimental or self-pitying: it is the truth for Hemingway about what it means to be alive—that each of us is dying. When we are young we believe otherwise, as does Nick Adams in trailing his hand in the warm water on a sharp chilly morning at the close of "Indian Camp," the first story of *In Our Time* (1925): "In the early morning on the lake sitting in the stern of the boat with his father rowing, he felt quite sure that he would never die." The questions Hemingway confronted were these: Since finally we know that everyone dies, how should we live? Why should we live?

For Hemingway these questions do not depend upon God. Not for him is the promise of the New Testament: "the last enemy that shall be destroyed is death" (I Corinthians 15:26). Hemingway wrote against death; he professed that his best sentences could embody a feeling forever even as he knew that this forever could never be forever. A great book is a postponement of the inevitable: there is no defense against Time's scythe. If you think that something will last forever, you are not looking far enough ahead. It is punitive to think in such terms, which is why Hemingway often claimed that his work might win an eternal life after all. It was pretty to think so.

Facing eternity, or the lack of it, each day, Hemingway wrote until he could write no longer, and then, in July 1961, he killed himself. He kept going after *The Old Man and the Sea*, but the thousands of pages of sentences and half-sentences he produced would not cohere as books and that was because he had nothing left to say. Santiago was inherent in the Nick Adams of "Indian Camp," in the frailty of the overinsistent "quite sure" that he would never die. In *The Old Man and the Sea*, Hemingway gave life to the character that was always waiting for him, the person whom in a sense he always was, even when he was a handsome young man in his twenties, full of promise in Paris. A friend of his first wife, Hadley Richardson, remembered him: "You wouldn't believe what a beautiful youth Ernest was. . . . He laughed aloud a lot from quick humor and from sheer joy in being alive." It is miraculous that this writer lasted as long as he did. He wrote with a gun to his head every day.

I have not yet done justice to *The Old Man and the Sea*. This novel is more extreme than I have suggested—than I even want to suggest. It has an unyielding power in its scenes and in its vision that expose dimensions of experience that are almost impossible to face and that bring home with intensity the feelings that Hemingway explored. When the sentences of *The Old Man and the Sea* are lingered over, the experience of the novel becomes unforgettable and unforgiving: it wounds the reader's consciousness. This novel's extremity is evident early in the action, as Santiago prepares for a new day of fishing: "The successful fishermen of that day were already in and had butchered their marlin out and carried them laid full length across two planks, with two men staggering at the end of each plank, to the fish house where they waited for the ice truck to carry them to the market in Havana. Those who had caught sharks had taken them to the shark factory on the other side of the cove where they were hoisted on a block and tackle, their livers removed, their fins cut off and their hides skinned out and their flesh cut into strips for salting."

The verb *butchered* describes the activity of preparing the marlin for sale but carries with it the connotation of unflinching slaughter, which Hemingway amplifies in the final sentence, with its hoisting, removing, cutting, and skinning. The impact is visceral and is meant to elide differences between marlins and sharks and human beings. Hemingway makes us remember that we are as permeable as are these creatures; our flesh is vulnerable to the knife—we can be cut to pieces—and our bodies will be degraded too. The humiliations of lifelessness are contained in us.

Hemingway was a fisherman, hunter, ambulance driver, war reporter, soldier; he was wounded and injured countless times and knew what a knife could do. The rending of bodies appears throughout his nonfiction reportage on wars and battles (journalism is one-third of his total output) and in his fiction from the woman in "Indian Camp" whom Nick's father sews up after the Caesarean and her husband who cuts his throat from ear to ear to the mutilated Jake Barnes, the bloodied Frederic Henry and the hemorrhaging Catherine Barkley, and the wounded, broken down, dying, or dead figures of Harry Morgan, Robert Jordan, Colonel Cantwell, and Thomas Hudson.

"Gee I was sorry when I heard that you were to go under the knife," Hemingway wrote to his sister Marcelline, May 20, 1921, after she had told him about an operation ahead. "There's nothing bothers me like having a dear old friend or relative go under the knife," he says again in this letter, and he repeats the phrase "under the knife" eight more times before he is done. Hemingway truly was his father Dr. Clarence E. Hemingway's son: cutting was in his blood.

The blood flows in *The Old Man and Sea*, as when Manolin recalls his first boat trip with Santiago: "I can remember the tail slapping and banging and the thwart breaking and the noise of the clubbing. I can remember you throwing me into the bow where the wet coiled lines were and feeling the whole boat shiver and the noise of you clubbing him like chopping a tree down and the sweet blood smell all over me."

To my ear the phrase "the wet coiled lines" does not fall within the range of Manolin's voice. Neither does "feeling the whole boat shiver." The rhythm is right for Hemingway himself, whereas for Manolin it is instead the phrase "the noise of you clubbing him" that expresses how he would speak. Hemingway wants it this way: his voice resonates within the voice of the character he is presenting; his voice is in the midst of his character's words. We will miss the power of the scene if we fail to see how subtle and intimate it is. It affirms companionship that partakes of repulsion and joy, bloody and sweet.

A later sequence of sentences, describing Santiago's baits, extends and toughens this pointed piteous effect: "Each bait hung head down with the shank of the hook inside the bait fish, tied and sewed solid and all the projecting part of the hook, the curve and the point, was covered with fresh sardines. Each sardine was hooked through both eyes so that they made a half-garland on the projecting steel. There was no part of the hook that a great fish could feel which was not sweet smelling and good tasting."

Feel the hook passing through your eyes. The helplessness of each fish, the mutilation inflicted upon it, show us what we are capable of and do all the time: this is what we do to fish, and what throughout history human beings have done to one another. Santiago enjoys his occupation; he is an expert. The fish he hopes to catch is "great" literally and figuratively, and its meat and blood are sweet. The play of light, the salt smell in the breeze, the endurance of this aged fisherman—the scene is seductive yet horrific, calling to mind Oedipus gouging his eyes in Sophocles' play and the tormentors in *King Lear* who bind the corky arms of Gloucester and grind his eyes to sightlessness.

The Old Man and the Sea is a theater of cruelty with a flesh-piercing array of images and terms that complicate the novel's renderings of nature's wonder and humankind's courage. One could characterize *The Old Man and the Sea*, as some have done, as an existentialist novel, but while the writings of existential philosophers such as Jean-Paul Sartre and Albert Camus offer contrast and comparison, they are not directly relevant to the inquiry that Hemingway undertook: he came to questions of life and death on his own and was brooding over them when he was in his teens. He forged his style by studying Sherwood Anderson, Gertrude Stein, and James Joyce, among others, even as he developed his conceptions of identity and nature within the contexts of his family, his hometown of Oak Park, Illinois, with its schools and churches, his summers in Michigan, and his experiences in love and war.

Here is Santiago thinking about the "big sea turtles": "Most people are heartless about turtles because a turtle's heart will beat for hours after he has been cut up and butchered. But the old man thought, I have such a heart too and my feet and hands are like theirs." The first sentence records a fact that at first makes no sense: one might have expected the sight of the turtle's heart continuing to beat after it is slaughtered to lead us to be the opposite of "heartless." It is a grotesque image; if you read the sentence, it will stay with you. We are heartless when we see this sight because we have no hearts ourselves. But Santiago says that he does and that his hands and feet are turtlelike; he is one of them. If at this moment he is different from us, it is because at this moment he is not human.

If he is human, it is because he is a killer. As the marlin eats the bait, Santiago says: "Eat it so that the point of the hook goes into your heart and kills you, he thought. Come up easy and let me put the harpoon into you. All right. Are you ready? Have you been long enough at table?" His tone is beguiling and ruthless; he loves his prey heartlessly. The domesticity of the marlin "at table" makes the scene more dreadful: Santiago's love for the marlin coincides with his intention to kill it. He kills the creature he loves, and he loves it because he can and will kill it.

Once the marlin is hooked, Santiago cuts away one line and connects it to "the two reserve coils": "It was difficult in the dark and once the fish made a surge that pulled him down on his face and made a cut below his eye. The blood ran down his cheek a little way." The "him" refers to Santiago, but for a second we interpret it as the fish because this is the noun that has come just before. The pronoun *him* is the fish and is Santiago too, who has cut the fish but who now is bloodied himself, like the sardines hooked through the eyes, and like the fish clubbed until its sweet blood covers Manolin.

To give himself strength, Santiago eats pieces of tuna: "Holding the line with his left shoulder again, and bracing on his left hand and arm, he took the tuna off the gaff hook and put the gaff back in place. He put one knee on the fish and cut strips of dark red meat longitudinally from the back of the head to the tail. They were wedge-shaped strips and he cut them from next to the back bone down to the edge of the belly.... I wish I could feed the fish, he thought. He is my brother. But I must kill him and keep strong to do it. Slowly and conscientiously he ate all of the wedge-shaped strips of fish."

"Brother" implies one level of relationship, but this bond evolves toward a deeper one that declares Santiago's identity with his prey, an identity to which Hemingway testifies in sentences as the novel moves toward its climax and conclusion: "But I must get him close, close, close, he thought. I mustn't try for the head. I must get the heart." "The shaft of the harpoon was projecting at an angle from the fish's shoulder and the sea was discolouring with the red of the blood from his heart.... I think I felt his heart," he thought. "He did not want to look at the fish. He knew that half of him had been destroyed. . . . He liked to think of the fish and what he could do to a shark if he were swimming free." The killing of the marlin is savage and heartbreaking, brutal and erotic. By killing the fish he loves, Santiago becomes one with it as the ambiguous "half of him had been destroyed" suggests. It is not just that he has taken life, but also that he has experienced what it is like to die.

In Hemingway's work it is unclear whether it is more painful to die or more painful to live. The wrenching pain of life is signified in *The Old Man and the Sea* when Santiago sees two sharks approaching the boat: "'*Ay*,' he said aloud. There is no translation for this word and perhaps it is just a noise such as a man might make, involuntarily, feeling the nail go through his hands and into the wood." There is no translation for this word because the feeling knows no bounds: no language, not Spanish or English or any other, can name it. It may not even be a word but, rather, a "noise," an expression of utterly helpless incoherence.

Nowhere in the accounts of the Crucifixion in the Gospel narratives is mention made of nails going through Jesus' hands and into the wood of the cross. Nailing, however, rather than binding with rope, was a common practice, and the story of Thomas's doubt of Jesus' resurrection (John 20:24–31) is keyed to his desire to see and feel "the print of the nails." For Hemingway, the nails are crucial, so much so that I am almost tempted to say we should not dwell upon the Crucifixion of Jesus itself when we read Hemingway's lines, but, instead, imagine as acutely as we can the word we would cry out or the noise we would make if it were our hands through which nails were driven. "My wounds were now hurting," Hemingway said in a letter to his parents (August 18, 1918) after he had been wounded, "like 227 little devils were driving nails into the raw."

We know that Hemingway was captivated by representations of Jesus on the cross and pondered them often. The image figures, for example, in many paintings by the Old Masters he revered and examined in the Louvre, the Prado, and other museums. "Lots of nail holes," says Frederic Henry about Andrea Mantegna in *A Farewell to Arms*, alluding to Mantegna's *The Lamentation over the Dead Christ* (c. 1490), a painting in the Brera National Art Gallery in Milan, where in the summer and fall of 1918 the nineteen-year-old Hemingway recovered from the wounds he described in his letter to his parents. He was haunted by bodies pierced, lacerated, and cut, in anguish like the body of the crucified Jesus.

In Madrid in mid-May 1926, Hemingway wrote a short story entitled "Today Is Friday," which presents the conversation of three Roman soldiers late in the evening of the day of the Crucifixion. The second soldier wants to know why Jesus did not come down from the cross, and the first soldier replies that Jesus did not want to—"that's not his play." The second soldier insists that everyone wants to come down from the cross: "Show me one that doesn't want to get down off the cross when the time comes." "What I mean is," he continues, "when the time comes. When they first start nailing him, there isn't none of them wouldn't stop it if they could." The third soldier then says, "The part I don't like is the nailing them on. You know, that must get to you pretty bad." Hemingway uses his pronouns keenly: Is "you" the person being nailed, or the person watching the nailing, or the person watching who feels as if he is being nailed himself? Or is the "you" intended above all to wound the reader, impelling each of us to imagine how we would feel if we were nailed to a cross?

Later Santiago shoulders the mast as he walks ashore, and soon he rests on his bed with "his arms out straight and the palms of his hands up." Santiago is the crucified Jesus, by which I mean that the pain he has gone through has taken him as close to the divine as any man can be. But the identification that matters is less with Jesus himself than, more specifically, with Jesus' pain—the weight of a cross cutting into the shoulder, the nails pounded through hands and feet, and above all this cry: "And about the ninth hour Jesus cried with a loud voice, saying, 'Eli, Eli, lama sabachthani?' that is to say, 'My God, My God, why hast thou forsaken me?'" (Matthew 27:46). Echoing the first line of Psalm 22, this is for me the most searing passage in the Gospels. It brings before us the voice of absolute abandonment, a pain no language or translation is adequate to, a question cast into a void. This is life at its most essential, as Hemingway understands it: forsaken man crucified, alone, emits an appeal to which there is no reply.

For Hemingway, Jesus was not the Redeemer but the peerless embodiment of a life of pain. Jesus accepted a mission: he knew he was dead the moment he was born. He embraced it freely because he knew that through his death was eternal life for all humankind. This is a promise of salvation in which Hemingway did not believe. For him there was no life after death, and his abiding concern increasingly came to be why and how a dying person—we are always dying—makes art. Santiago toward the end in fact wonders whether he might be "already dead," but then he realizes he "was not dead," and he knows he is not because he feels "pain." Pain confirms for the old man he is alive, and as long as he is alive, he works.

Hemingway's son John said after his father's death: "I keep thinking what a wonderful old man he would have made if he'd learned how. I don't think he had faced up to becoming old." Yet the pain cut deeper, as another of his sons, Gregory, suggested when he said his father lived "with the knowledge of what the edge of nothingness is like." It was not only what Hemingway could not face but also what he did face. Returning to the harbor, Santiago reflects: "And what beat you, he thought. 'Nothing', he said aloud. 'I went out too far.'" He pulls in the boat by himself because "there was no one to help him." Far out, Hemingway saw nothing and that was the vision that gives such desperation to the disciplined books he wrote. As he said two years later in his Nobel Prize acceptance speech, he had made a commitment to be a writer "driven far out past where he can go, to where no one can help him."

Hemingway realized he wanted from his sentences more than sentences in books, however great, could give. For this reason I think he did not care much about his books once they were done. What Hemingway cherished was the act of writing them, the experience of making them—of moving his pencil across the page, of making, revising, and honing sentences. In the introduction he wrote in 1948 for a new edition of *A Farewell to Arms*, he explained what it felt like to write this novel:

> I remember living in the book and making up what happened in it every day. Making the country and the people and the things that happened I was happier than I had ever been. Each day I read the book through from the beginning to the point where I went on writing and each day I stopped when I was still going good and when I knew what would happen next. The fact that the book was a tragic one did not make me unhappy since I believed that life was a tragedy and knew it could only have one end. But finding you were able to make something up; to create truly enough so that it made you happy to read it; and to do this every day you worked was something that gave a greater pleasure than any I had ever known. Beside it nothing else mattered.

Inside the world of the book while it was being written, it was possible for Hemingway to feel nothing else mattered, including the reality of death. This for him was the thrill of creation—a form of happiness oblivious to its own impermanence. In the midst of his sentences as he wrote them, Hemingway could experience the feeling of immortality: I am not immortal but, at this moment, I feel as if I were. But when the final sentence was written and the book was done, where was he? What next?

He would have to attempt to do it again, writing himself into a place where nothing mattered. He knew all the time that his story could only have one end.

Hunting, Fishing, and the Cramp of Ethics in Ernest Hemingway's *The Old Man and the Sea, Green Hills of Africa,* and *Under Kilimanjaro*

Ryan Hediger

Ryan Hediger is an assistant professor of English at La Salle University.

In the following viewpoint, Ryan Hediger writes about the evolution of Ernest Hemingway's attitude about hunting. Several critics have pointed out that in later books, Hemingway seems content to watch wildlife, not kill it. Hediger suggests that Hemingway's affinity for the natural world was a part of his abiding search for a code of ethics and right living.

Toward the end of Hemingway's second African safari (1953–54), he took up his own version of a traditional Masai practice: hunting alone at night, barefoot, head shaved, and carrying only a spear. These walks are described in *Under Kilimanjaro* (2005) (and in the abridged *True at First Light,* 1999). Both versions reveal, with some self-deprecating humor, that Hemingway was "properly scared" and wished for any kind of companion, dog or human. Yet, he calls that fear "a luxury that you have to pay for and like the best luxuries it is worth it most of the time" (*TAFL* 271; *UK* 361). As the description proceeds, we understand that the reward is a complex experience of the African night, including the sounds of "night birds," "small animals," and a lion; the sight of foxes,

Ryan Hediger, "Hunting, Fishing, and the Cramp of Ethics in Ernest Hemingway's *The Old Man and the Sea, Green Hills of Africa,* and *Under Kilimanjaro,*" *Hemingway Review,* vol. 27, no. 2, Spring 2008, p. 35. Copyright © 2008 by The Hemingway Review. All rights reserved. Reproduced by permission.

hares, a wildebeest, and more; and a clearer sense of himself as another animal, exposed to that sweating fear. It is tempting to call this reward aesthetic, at least in part.

Many readers note that such practices also have an ethical valence, especially in comparison to Hemingway's first safari (1933–34), depicted in *Green Hills of Africa*. Introducing *Under Kilimanjaro*, for instance, editors Robert W. Lewis and Robert E. Fleming mention Hemingway's changed attitude toward hunting, saying he "takes greater pleasure in merely watching the wildlife" than in killing (xiv). In a recent article, "'He Only Looked Sad the Same Way I Felt': The Textual Confessions of Hemingway's Hunters," Carey Voeller also demonstrates that Hemingway showed more and more sympathy toward animals on later trips, replacing his trophy-hunting mentality with a more complex view. For Voeller, these changes are part of a general shift in Hemingway's later life. Voeller's argument follows from Charlene Murphy's work, which he cites, and resembles a number of other studies that draw similar conclusions on this point.[1]

Not mentioned in Voeller's study but also relevant to this issue is Glen Love's 1987 essay "Hemingway's Indian Virtues." Love condemns excessive killing in Hemingway's personal hunting practices (e.g. 203) and finds Hemingway's Santiago in *The Old Man and the Sea* also too willing to kill the sharks and other animals of the sea that oppose his interests. However, Love notes signs of Hemingway's shift toward greater ecological benevolence "at about the time of the writing" of *The Old Man and the Sea* (209). As he reminds us, by this time Hemingway had published his belief that "it is a sin to kill any non-dangerous game animal except for meat" (qtd. in Love 209) and had spoken against other wanton killing. Love seems to deduce this as a kind of moral code for Hemingway's later hunting practices.

Love's analysis contrasts this growing sympathy with animals with Hemingway's status "as a modern and as an artist," a maker—"proclaiming of his own uniqueness, [which] also necessitated a destruction or diminishment of the natural world which he loved [. . .]" (205). For Love, artistic style conflicts with ethics. On this point, Love's approach resembles critical arguments heard not long after release of *The Old Man and the Sea*. Although the novel was greeted with high praise at first, a second wave of responses was more skeptical. Philip Rahv, for example, calls the story "supple" and "exact" but also finds it limited because of Hemingway's "chosen theme" (360). Rahv suggests that "its quality of emotion [is] genuine but so elemental in its totality as to exact nothing from us beyond instant assent" (360). Philip Young praised the book highly in his first edition of *Ernest Hemingway* (1952), but in the 1966 edition notes his desire to "greatly tone down the praise for *The Old Man and the Sea*." He proclaims that "although the tale is here and there exciting it is itself drawn out a little far. Even the title seems an affectation of simplicity, and the realization that Hemingway was now trading on and no longer inventing the style that made him famous came just too late" to Young, hence his initially high praise (274). Young heartily agrees with Dwight Macdonald, who wrote, "'Nothing is at stake [in *The Old Man and the Sea*] except for the professional obligation to sound as much like Hemingway as possible'" (qtd. in Young 271–72). Indeed, Young uses this discussion to reflect his belief in "the declination of Hemingway's powers—physical, mental, hence literary" (264). Such views all turn on the idea that the story's theme is insignificant and that Hemingway's use of his characteristic style is a form of "fakery," to borrow Robert Weeks's term. Style is at odds with serious, sincere writing in this critical framework.

This notion of internal conflict recalls other, more recent critical accounts insofar as they understand Hemingway to embody, in Voeller's concluding words, "contradictory and very human ideas" (75). Murphy argues that Hemingway could both love and kill animals, recasting this apparent contradiction as a "duality." Similarly, as Lewis and Fleming mark Hemingway's decreased interest in killing animals late in life, as mentioned above, they suggest he took "pleasure" in watching animals instead. This word choice begs the question of what motivates this change (although clearly, unlike earlier critics, these readers find the theme of such works valuable). Has Hemingway merely substituted the pleasure of watching for the pleasure of killing, without significantly considering the interests of other forms of life? How are we to understand "pleasure" here? Or to frame the question more broadly, what relationship does aesthetic engagement, including experiential pleasure, have to ethics? Should we content ourselves with the familiar but unsatisfying notion that Hemingway's work and conduct regarding animals is complex because it is contradictory?

This essay approaches this problem by revising what we mean by "ethics," permitting us to find an important and principled consistency—one that develops more fully as time passes—in Hemingway's conduct toward and writing about animals. While many critics of Hemingway's treatment of animals—Love, for example—suppose some clear-cut ethical principle against which that treatment can be measured, I rely on recent theory presenting ethics as centered on openness to experience and to aesthetics. In this approach, ethical principles are subject to change based on local conditions of time and place; ethical principles and human actors are thus more fully in dialogue. Hemingway's rigorous attention to particulars and his lifelong stance against abstraction are therefore fundamental to his sense of ethics.

After exploring these points about ethics with reference to the safari books *Green Hills of Africa* and *Under Kilimanjaro*, this essay will examine *The Old Man and the Sea* to show its presentation of ethics as a rigorous, ongoing process. Santiago does not decide upon his ethical stance towards the marlin until he has undergone the encounter. But more crucially for my argument, the novel's rigorous attention to style, to aesthetics, highlights the importance of something like deep inhabitation. The style of *The Old Man and the Sea* conveys Santiago's keen, embodied awareness of the Cuban marine environment and its life, and that awareness is not only valuable in itself, but fundamentally informs his ethical considerations. Crucially, this form of ethics is not some rote application of a rule about never killing animals. Hemingway is fully aware of the fact that eating requires killing. Rather, this paper argues that in Hemingway's later texts, dead animals—the number of trophies, the size of their horns, or the weight of their flesh— become less necessary as a measure or memento of his hunting or fishing experience, and ethical experience itself takes greater emphasis.

Sport and Ethics

The safari presented in *Green Hills of Africa* can seem merely a masculine contest in killing power, measured in simple terms such as the sheer numbers of animals killed or the size of their horns. The book's ethics would therefore involve not shooting animals from moving vehicles, obeying license requirements, and doing one's best to be civilized in the midst of the struggle to best one's hunting companions. The primary plot line of *Green Hills of Africa* consists of a competition between Karl and the Hemingway-figure narrator for size and quality of trophies, while the book's subplot is a literary competition between forms of writing. Hemingway announces this literary competition in the foreword: "The writer has attempted to write an absolutely true book to see whether the shape of a country and the pattern of a month's action can, if truly presented, *compete* with a work of the imagination" (my emphasis). In the literary asides that recur through the book, Hemingway develops this element into a justification for the nonfiction form he is practicing.

But winning such competitions is not the book's highest value. Hemingway, although he presents himself as more skilled than Karl, loses the battle of the trophies consistently and finally (e.g. *GHOA* 63, 83, 86, 153, 291, and passim). He also admits to himself and to readers that M'Cola, one of the African hunters, "was immeasurably the better man and the better tracker" (269). The literary competition also proves difficult to resolve as victory or defeat; the distinction between a work of the imagination and an "absolutely true book" erodes when Hemingway expresses his aspiration not only as wanting "to try to write something about the country and the animals and what it's like to someone who knows nothing about it," but also to evoke how he and his companions "feel about the country," to indicate "the way we feel about it" (194). This kind of talk about "feel" pushes the nonfiction form back toward fiction or narrative, and without an absolute distinction between forms, how can we say one form has bested the other?

In all of these cases throughout *Green Hills of Africa*, the framework of competition modulates into something more complex, focused always on experiences of the country and their value. Acknowledging this point permits us to revisit Hemingway's conflict with himself about the animals he shoots and his desire to beat Karl. For instance, near the end of the book when he is pursuing sable, Hemingway explains, "I did not mind killing anything, any animal, if I killed it cleanly," because he "ate the meat and kept the hides and horns" (*GHOA* 272) and therefore did not waste the animal's life. But, Hemingway continues, he "felt rotten sick over this sable bull" because "I wanted him damned badly, I wanted him more than I would admit" (272). Read strictly in terms of the plot about competition, Hemingway feels sick about the intensity of his desire because it is ungentlemanly.

But this internal conflict must also be read in terms of what the animals signify outside of human-to-human competition. Again and again, members of the safari note the beauty of the animals they kill. Poor Old Momma, to cite one example, says of a rhino Hemingway shoots, "Didn't he look wonderful going along there?" (*GHOA* 77). Cognizance of the paradox of killing to preserve should be read back into Hemingway's reluctance to admit how much he wants, for example, to find and kill the sable. The nature of this paradox becomes clearer by the end of the book, when Hemingway expresses his wish to return to Africa with more time to "get to know it as I knew the country around the lake where we were brought up" (*GHOA* 282). On this return trip he would "see the buffalo feeding where they lived, and when elephants came through the hills we would see them and watch them breaking branches and not have to shoot [. . .]." He would be able to "see them long enough so they belonged to me forever," without always having to kill them (*GHOA* 282). The animal trophies are only imperfect mementos, standing against the flight of time and the necessity of leaving the place; they are imperfect replacements, like narratives or other such texts, for experience itself, which is the real value.

When Hemingway falters on the thin satisfaction of the trophy as a supplement for ongoing experience, what arises is an interrogation of the larger life conditions that make trophies seem desirable in the first place. That is why his critique of the trophy mentality, already developing in *Green Hills of Africa*, amounts not to some simple rule about killing animals, but to a whole system of regard for place, inhabitation, and animals. At stake is the way he lives in the world. Suzanne del Gizzo, working with *True at First Light* before the release of *Under Kilimanjaro*, makes a similar point about Hemingway's second safari. She suggests that this text shows how, in Africa, he "may have been seeking to become a member of a culture without writers—a place where he would have the opportunity to explore himself and re-define his identity on other terms" (518). In other words, Hemingway wanted to inhabit the place seriously more than he wanted to produce artifacts (like texts, or trophies) about brief visits.

This anti-product orientation is already visible in *Green Hills of Africa,* visible even in the often-discussed rebuke of the "foreigner," who "destroys, cuts down the trees, drains the water [. . .]" and so on (*GHOA* 284). This famous critique opens with the observation that "A continent ages quickly once we come," its first person plural ("we come") self-consciously positioning Hemingway squarely and self-consciously within the colonialist behavior he challenges and justifying his unease about participating in the trophy-hunting safari (284). Within this critique of colonialism are further signs of this book's often conflicted discourse. Immediately following this searing comment is Hemingway's insistence that he "would come back to Africa" and that "*we* always had the right to go somewhere else" (285, my emphasis). Such points are more than contradictory. They foreground the fact that we always inherit subject positions that are, to some extent, beyond our control, that we are often complicit in realities we did not choose, and that we must work to recognize who and what we are if we are to make ethical choices. The narrative in *Green Hills of Africa* presents Hemingway at least partly coming to terms with the system he inhabits, experiencing an uneasiness, a kind of cramp of ethical feeling.

In the second safari, Hemingway extends and solidifies many of the lessons he learned on the first safari, constantly underscoring the value of deep inhabitation. In a key passage, he does so explicitly, and as is often the case in his work, he writes about his awareness of place in terms of the animals who live there:

> I thought how lucky we were this time in Africa to be living long enough in one place so that we knew the individual animals and knew the snake holes and the snakes that lived in them. When I had first been to Africa we were always in a hurry to move from one place to another to hunt beasts for

> trophies. If you saw a cobra it was an accident as it would
> be to find a rattler on the road in Wyoming. Now we knew
> many places where cobras lived. (*UK* 116; *TAFL* 97–98)

This more local and particular awareness seems tied to the claim he makes in the next paragraph: "The time of shooting beasts for trophies was long past with me." Instead, he "was shooting for the meat we needed to eat and to back up Miss Mary and against beasts that had been outlawed for cause [. . .]" (TAFL 98; UK 117). Although the paragraph goes on to mention an impala that he did in fact shoot "for trophy," Hemingway clearly marks out a critique of wasteful killing here, as critics have suggested. In place of the recreational pursuit of animals that is trophy hunting, Hemingway emphasizes his engaged knowledge of place and his experiences. These experiences, like the strange pleasures of walking at night, are more aesthetic and qualitative than the more easily calculated, quantitative successes in killing.

These two systems of evaluating safari trips provide useful examples for thinking about ethics more generally. In the trophy-hunting system, ethics are essentially rules that permit the game of competition among humans to proceed. There are rules about how to kill animals and about how many animals can be killed, and more subtle expectations about decency toward one's fellow competitors. The rules are more or less fixed, and the hunters simply follow them. The system ostensibly values animals insofar as they cannot be heedlessly slaughtered, but not much beyond that, and views the environment as a backdrop for a human endeavor. Hemingway inhabited this approach to animals and to hunting uneasily even on his first safari. On the second safari, advances in his thinking about inhabiting place register in a relatively minor shift regarding the ethics of killing animals—he will do so only for meat. But this specific principle is only the tip of his ethical iceberg. The less visible portions of this structure involve a thorough awareness of what it means to be one among many mortal animals in a larger ecology, one consequence of his deep inhabitation. Indeed, it is partly the mortality we share with animals that renders our encounters with them meaningful.

Although there is not space to explore this notion fully here, our ever-present need to eat is a sign of our corporeality and mortality, a sign of human limitation that heightens Hemingway's desire to attend to experience carefully. He constantly feels time passing. With such cognizance, Hemingway treats animals neither as pawns in a human competition, nor as beings so entirely foreign that he believes himself outside of the natural economy in which life depends upon other forms of life. Thus, he continues to hunt and kill animals for food.

This account of ethics, which distinguishes following a rule from having a sensibility open to experience, may sound somewhat strained given that Hemingway can simply be understood to follow a rule—only kill animals for meat. But such a view of ethics mistakes the role of the ethical agent, who, for Hemingway and for theorists like Jacques Derrida, must take greater responsibility for being ethical than simply following rules. Moreover, this paper's approach to ethics permits people in a different context than Hemingway's to reach different conclusions about hunting. For example, knowing how overfished today's oceans are, an individual might decide to avoid killing fish even to eat them, at least until populations recover.

This second system of ethical regard refuses to separate the agent from the ethical system, so that Hemingway must constantly revisit the principles with which he confronts animals and places.

The first system, one in which a set of ideas or rules is generally stable, is a more familiar notion of ethics to many of us. The agent's task is simply to obey (or disobey) that system. Hemingway was famously suspicious of such abstract systems of understanding.[2] His work on this point resembles later critiques of ethical systems in law, religion, and other fundamental doctrines. Geoffrey Galt Harpham explains that such critiques, which gathered force in the 1960s, understood conventional ethical systems as merely "rendering mystical and grand their [creators'] own private interests or desires" (387). For instance, in the case of trophy hunting, the animal head or carcass would function as a sign of human prowess and mastery over nature in general. On safaris, trophies would reiterate the international hegemonic system, as the white European demonstrated his (or, less often, her) mastery over the nature of Africa, including both humans and animals. Implicit in this colonialist and imperialist view was, now quite infamously, a set of "ethical" implications, perhaps most egregiously expressed in the idea of the "white man's burden" to "civilize" non-Europeans.

Critiques of such misguided ethics have led to revised notions of what ethics might mean more generally, revisions often referred to as the "ethical turn" in contemporary examples. Philosophers like Emmanuel Levinas and later Jacques Derrida, who was influenced by Levinas, worked to revive or reform ethical discourses by shifting notions of ethics away from merely obeying pre-established codes. In their analyses, ethics must factor the complexities of experience into inherited codes and understandings. The defamiliarizing, often profoundly upsetting character of experience is discussed in Levinas's work, especially *Otherwise Than Being*, as exposure to the radical difference between self and other. Levinas's conception of these matters embodies the experience of ethics in the very viscera at times. Near the conclusion of *Otherwise Than Being*, for example, he writes that "the subject gives himself and exposes himself in his lungs, without intentions and aims, [. . .] the subject could be a lung at the bottom of its substance" (180). In such accounts, we are exposed to the other in all of our dealings. The involuntary character of breathing thus serves as a figure for and example of ethical selfhood that we enter into without ever having decided to do so. We are immersed in a world that continually makes ethical demands upon us. For Levinas, only in such a conception can we practice the doubting of self and law that sincere ethical practice requires, sometimes going so far as to do the opposite of what cultural codes such as laws would command. Derrida has recently summarized this approach to ethics by saying that "casting doubt on responsibility, on decision, on one's own being-ethical" is at the center of ethics (128).[3]

Hemingway undertakes this type of endeavor in his barefoot night walks in Africa, becoming "properly scared" in order to experience the complexities of the place under Kilimanjaro. This embodied exposure to the radical otherness of night and of dangerous animals such as cobras and lions enriches his sensibility and his writing. Night walking therefore connects to a profoundly humbled sense of self at the level of the body. Hemingway deliberately immerses himself in a large and potentially dangerous world that dwarfs the meaning of the individual and presents new insights about how such a life might be lived. This ethical sensibility renders *Under Kilimanjaro* a book that Lewis and Fleming call "most lighthearted yet unconventionally serious" (*UK* viii), an apt description for much of Hemingway's work. The book reiterates the often intimate connection between art and life for Hemingway; writing was a way for him to draw new conclusions about how to live, or about ethics in general terms. As with *Green Hills of Africa*, the (mostly) nonfiction genre of *Under Kilimanjaro* marks Hemingway's seriousness in considering Africa, as the book works with actual events. But in *Under Kilimanjaro*, the encounter between Hemingway and Africa requires a new openness and receptivity on Hemingway's part, a kind of negative capability that is distinctly ethical in the sense described by Derrida and Levinas.

Yet Hemingway's idiosyncratic adoption of Masai practices can also be seen as a suspicious form of "going native," one for which he has been sharply criticized, especially in ethical terms. Toni Morrison, for instance, understands Hemingway's primitivism in books like *The Garden of Eden* to depend on a notion of Africa as a "blank, empty space into which he asserts himself" (88–89). I believe Morrison is at least partly right, as Hemingway himself was aware, and as I have argued, in the case of *Green Hills of Africa*. But I am also suggesting that to a significant extent, the opposite is true; Hemingway regarded himself as a partly blank page onto which Africa and African cultures could write themselves. In saying so, I do not mean to excuse each of Hemingway's actions so much as to indicate how his notion of ethics allows for cross-cultural and even human/nonhuman exchanges. Throughout his life, defamiliarization in foreign cultures and places seems to have helped him consider the rationales for ethical systems and work to formulate an ethical system of his own that was more than the mere abstractions he so disliked. Some of the nuances of his ethical sensibility appear in the carefully crafted presentation of Santiago, that "strange old man" (*OMATS* 66).

The Cramp of Ethics in *The Old Man and the Sea*

The Old Man and the Sea is a critique of triumphalist hunting. It unravels Santiago's apparently great victory at sea, delivering a mere skeleton for a trophy. Indeed, the marlin's skeleton signifies the impossibility of a trophy sufficient to represent either the living fish or Santiago's experience of the hunt and his knowledge of the sea. The skeleton trophy also suggests the error implicit in commodifying the sea and attempting to turn its life into product. Santiago, thoroughly knowledgeable about the local environment, understands and admits his error, and is ultimately forced to revise his ethical code: "'I shouldn't have gone out so far, fish,' he said. 'Neither for you nor for me. I'm sorry, fish'" (*OMATS* 110). By story's end, Santiago's own survival is in doubt as he is revealed to be on the edge of death.

Deliberately putting his person into a position of doubt, defamiliarizing himself in an environment he generally knows well, is a premise of Santiago's trip and of his fishing practice more broadly. As Susan Beegel has recently shown in "A Guide to the Marine Life in Ernest Hemingway's *The Old Man and the Sea*," Santiago is well-attuned to the otherness of the ocean and its animals. With rigorous detail, Beegel maps the ways in which Hemingway has, in minimalist fashion, rendered Santiago's knowledge of the sea. Beegel summarizes her findings by saying, "A few strokes of his [Hemingway's] pen sufficed to limn a lifetime of intimacy with the sea and its creatures [. . .]." (309). On the trip depicted in the book, Santiago has gone further out to sea than is common. The distance and his primitive gear expose him quite fully to the whims of the ocean, to his prey, and to the sharks. Beegel's essay clarifies the gravity of this danger, for example, in Santiago's encounter with the mako shark, which "could easily result in the destruction of Santiago's skiff and his death from injury or drowning" (265). In this respect, his trip resembles Hemingway's late-night walks in Africa. Both Santiago and Hemingway limit their abilities to exert agency, trading control for raw, direct, informative experience, registered on their bodies.

Hemingway's presentation of Santiago emphasizes the shock of difference with rigorously crafted writing in which elements of style evoke what cannot be properly described in direct language: Hemingway's iceberg principle. We might call this style "skeletal" in the context of *The Old Man and the Sea*. Such writing, using understatement, repetition, and the like, often conveys embodied experiences, so that a stylistically complex description testifies to the dissonance between actual, full-bodied experience and the craft or technology of representing it with language. This stylistic approach, exemplified below, often amounts to a claim of humility and is frequently described as a kind of ethic (e.g. Bickford Sylvester "Hemingway's Extended Vision"). But more than this, such

A painting depicting Santiago and his struggle to catch the elusive marlin in Ernest Hemingway's The Old Man and the Sea. *This painting hangs in the Hemingway House in Key West, Florida, where the author lived and wrote.* © Arco Images/Therin-Weise/Alamy.

style aligns with what Zoe Trodd has recently called a "politics of form" that reaches beyond what can easily be shown, acknowledging the difficulties of representation (Trodd 8). In Hemingway's carefully constructed contexts, the word, the trophy, and other such signs carry marks of their insufficiency to reproduce complex reality.[4]

The limitations of representation appear as part of a more general approach to subjectivity in *The Old Man and the Sea*, in which even inhabitation of the body is a sign of limited agency. The signature moment of weakness, doubt, and ethical consideration for the present discussion occurs as Santiago begins to tire in his fishing travail, his left hand cramping closed:

> He rubbed the cramped hand against his trousers and tried to gentle the fingers. But it would not open. Maybe it will open with the sun, he thought. Maybe it will open when the strong tuna is digested. If I have to have it, I will open it, cost whatever it costs. But I do not want to open it now by

force. Let it open by itself and come back of its own accord. After all I abused it much in the night when it was necessary to free and untie the various lines. (*OMATS* 60)

Santiago is neither completely at home in his body nor able to inhabit some disembodied self. His ethical position with regard to his left hand—"let it open by itself"—is driven by the implicit understanding that the hand will function best when its needs are acknowledged, whatever the desires of the organizing subject who would have it do as he pleases. Hand is to body here as self is to environment more generally in the story.

Hemingway's style reveals dissonance between systems of understanding, such as language or ethics, and local realities of place, including the individuals who live in those places and the systems they use. The appearance of Spanish phrases in *The Old Man and the Sea*, for example, recalls the particular, local conditions of his Cuban setting, marking the difference between actuality and Hemingway's textuality, meant to address a broader audience. Early on, for instance, we read that Manolin asks Santiago to "'Tell me about the great John J. McGraw.' He said Jota for J" (*OMATS* 22). This technique is used with even more significance in the key passage later in the text where Santiago ponders the significance of his left hand cramping: "I hate a cramp, he thought. It is a treachery of one's own body. It is humiliating before others to have a diarrhoea from ptomaine poisoning or to vomit from it. But a cramp, he thought of it as a *calambre*, humiliates oneself especially when one is alone" (61–62).

The otherness of the Spanish word *calambre* helps us notice how language is functioning more generally in the text. Santiago has already decided to let the hand open by itself, and this is what he ultimately does (*OMATS* 60). Thus, despite his avowed hatred of a cramp, Santiago *practices* a careful inhabitation of his body that recognizes the difference between his desire for its absolute strength and the reality of his human weakness and mortality. The claim to hate his cramp, then, appears as a kind of overstatement to vent spleen. While sometimes read as simple, macho posturing, Santiago's language acts in an almost opposite way, as a comfort. The function of such language within the dramatic space of the story, where Santiago speaks to no one but himself, is not to convey meaning but to help him cope with his bodily limitations. The passage about the cramped hand embodies a kind of cramp in meaning. Just as the strange word *calambre* shows the heterogeneity of Hemingway's language, mixing the local Spanish with English, the frustrations expressed in this passage show the space between Santiago the desiring person and Santiago the body. Ultimately, it is Santiago's ethical response to the otherness of his own body that enables his hand to function again.

Hemingway uses the key word "treachery" both to describe the cramp ("a treachery of one's own body") and to describe how the old man had hooked the fish ("through treachery," *OMATS* 50), likening the catching of the fish to the cramping of his own body. Neither form of exalting the self in this text—whether physical achievements like successful fishing or effective use of language—provides a way for the self to feel completely triumphant. Instead, craft, teaching, and ultimately love (relationships, in other words) fill the place of self-gratification.

The story reveals craft in a doubled fashion, where Hemingway's descriptions evoke both his own writing abilities and Santiago's knowledge of the sea, as many readers have observed. But it is essential to the story that craft does not show mastery so much as humble, serious engagement in long-term relationships. The following passage demonstrates the careful expression of discipline at a key moment, as Santiago surveys his surroundings just prior to hooking the marlin:

> He could not see the green of the shore now but only the tops of the blue hills that showed white as though they were

snow-capped and the clouds that looked like high snow mountains above them. The sea was very dark and the light made prisms in the water. The myriad flecks of the plankton were annulled now by the high sun and it was only the great deep prisms in the blue water that the old man saw now with his lines going straight down into the water that was a mile deep. (*OMATS* 40)

He is too far out to see the shore and in blue water, both of which suggest his entrance into the ocean wilderness. The tremendous otherness of the ocean is further signaled by the repetitions of "deep" and "water" in a sentence crossed through with marks of sharp visual observation and practiced physical craft. Santiago is simultaneously shown both as knowledgeable and as relatively insignificant, with a sense of insignificance actually heightened by his knowledge. The paratactical style, clauses linked by "ands" and therefore not sorted hierarchically, conjures these things together. Thus qualifiers like "myriad" and "great" align with "straight" to encourage us to see how Santiago's accurate fishing derives from and grammatically parallels his awareness of the unfathomable otherness of the ocean. Appreciating the greatness of the sea is keeping straight lines.[5]

What I see here as admiring understatement may appear to other readers as fulsome description. Harold Bloom calls the book "overwritten" in a brief, dismissive introduction to a recollection of critical essays on the story. Put into the context of Hemingway's oeuvre, though, we can see understatement in *The Old Man and the Sea* partly by recognizing the effects of its style, which is perhaps *more* technically achieved than, for example, this passage from *The Sun Also Rises* celebrated by Larzer Ziff in "The Social Basis of Hemingway's Style":

In the morning it was bright, and they were sprinkling the streets of the town, and we all had breakfast in a café. Bayonne is a nice town. It is like a very clean Spanish town and it is on a river. Already, so early in the morning, it was very hot on the bridge across the river. We walked out on the bridge and then took a walk through the town. (*SAR* 90, quoted in Ziff 147)

Ziff points out how Jake Barnes is able to celebrate the café in Bayonne in *The Sun Also Rises* with doubled intensity because he so underwrites the praise. Jake is an exile looking for a culture and a life that seems truer to him. But the passage from *The Old Man and the Sea* quoted earlier is more subtle and has larger implications. It answers to Jake's old problem with a similar technique, showing Santiago's cultured life-practice as an ethical and loving inhabitation of place, but then it goes beyond simply investing that place with mere familiarity. The stylized description in *The Old Man and the Sea*, furthermore, with its rhythmic repetition of simple words like "deep" and "water," makes familiar language strange as well. Hemingway inhabits language as Santiago inhabits the sea.

Recognizing the importance of Santiago's place-awareness is crucial to understanding the function of style in this book more generally. Place-awareness bears, for instance, on another surprising innovation in Hemingway's work at the level of the word in this text. When introducing Manolin, he permits a key abstract term to enter the story directly, in a way he often avoided and or criticized in earlier books: "The old man had taught the boy to fish and the boy loved him" (10). This plain statement, early in the book, might seem simply to state what would be shown by superior art, making it perhaps less surprising that Bloom and others see the book as "sentimental," as relying on "emotion in excess of its object" (Bloom 3).

But I do not think Hemingway has simply lost control of his language here, or, to quote another critic, "gone soft."[6] Rather, this phrase functions as understatement because its brief revelation of Santiago and Manolin's relationship is balanced against the long, fatally trying fishing trip in solitude. The phrase depends greatly on the full context of the book.

The brief exchanges with Manolin locate Santiago in a human culture, but the fishing trip locates culture in a broader world of other species and of the ocean. The extent and importance of the nonhuman in this novel is signaled both by the length of the fishing account and by Santiago's persistent longing for Manolin's help. In this context, the sentiment of love, stated with ironic simplicity, signifies a human lineage that continues despite the mortal limitations of the individual. Again, "The old man had taught the boy to fish and the boy loved him" (10).

Moreover, the importance of ethical human relationships with the nonhuman seems entirely ignored in arguments like Bloom's, which do not acknowledge the value of this theme (instead, we saw Bloom claiming that the book shows "emotion in excess of its object," in keeping with other critics mentioned above). Beegel's guide to the marine life in this book sharpens our awareness of these different interpretive frameworks. She explains that although recent criticism by Glen Love, Gerry Brenner, Lisa Tyler, and Beegel herself responds to "the biocentrisim of *The Old Man and the Sea*," this critical work nonetheless "has been largely humanistic, proceeding from the political ideologies of environmentalism and ecofeminism" and the like (236). Her guide, however, is meant to investigate the marine science in Hemingway's book much more closely, more independently of political or philosophical ideologies. And in this sense, Beegel explains, she follows more carefully what Hemingway had in mind when writing the book. She quotes Hemingway arguing against excessively symbolic readings of the text, for instance, claiming, "'The sea is the sea. The old man is an old man. The boy is a boy and the fish is a fish. The sharks are all sharks, no better and no worse'" (Beegel 239–240). Hemingway, like many ecocritics who read him, including Beegel, Love, and myself, believed there was enough value in narrating the interactions between humanity and marine life to make such a story important, without the need for every natural fact to appear as a humanistic symbol of some other reality. This approach humbles the position of humanity while elevating the value of nonhuman nature.

Hemingway's anti-symbolic stance, if perhaps slightly overstated, highlights his sense of the intrinsic value of the sea and the marlin. Nonetheless, although Santiago respects the fish immensely, he also must eat. This places him in an ethical conundrum that, under the pressure of trauma and exhaustion as the story proceeds, leads to an essential inversion. After the cramps in his hand have been bothering him, and after the fish has shown itself by jumping, Santiago thinks, "I wish I could show him what sort of man I am. But then he would see the cramped hand. Let him think I am more man than I am and I will be so. I wish I was the fish, he thought [. . .]" (*OMATS* 64). Identity in this sequence of sentences moves from an expression of desire to a fiction. The desire—"I wish I could show him what sort of man I am"—is undercut by a realistic awareness of his cramped old body, and that awareness inspires a fiction told to the fish by the well-handled line—"Let him think I am more man than I am and I will be so." Like speaking aloud to himself, this fiction organizes and drives Santiago's activity. Santiago does not believe it to be true so much as potentially true from a certain perspective. But significantly, this acknowledgment of the fiction or performativity of the self, not only confirms that self, but also drives Santiago's desire to travel further outside of it. He wants to become the fish. This desire is crucial to a new awareness of his limits, to his sense that he should not have gone out so far.

This pattern is replayed and its significance extended over the next several pages, as Santiago's exhaustion grows. After contemplating the size and strength of the fish, he insists,

"I'll kill him though," he said. "In all his greatness and his glory." Although it is unjust, he thought. But I will show him what a man can do and what a man endures.

"I told the boy I was a strange old man," he said. "Now is when I must prove it."

The thousand times that he had proved it meant nothing. Now he was proving it again. Each time was a new time and he never thought about the past when he was doing it.

I wish he'd sleep and I could sleep and dream about the lions, he thought. Why are the lions the main thing that is left? (*OMATS* 66)

This dialogue swings wildly from position to position, even alternating between words spoken aloud to the self and internal dialogue. The first spoken words make a brave claim that Santiago hopes to live up to—"'I'll kill him'"—but the thoughts, like an internalized Greek chorus, immediately undercut the spoken words.[7] The "thousand times" paragraph reasserts his purpose, but more quietly than the first claim. By the time we reach the "I wish" response, the fiction of the self has again modulated into a surrender to the animal other and a desire for dreaming that is a key to the story.

The dream motif evokes the individual's unconscious and so marks the limits of will and control. The motif also softens or "gentles" the depiction of the self's limits (to echo Hemingway's terms from the book). Thus, although the central action of *The Old Man and the Sea* can appear to be a trauma, the story's recourse to the involuntary appeal of animal dreams, like the pleasures of Hemingway's style, shows ethical intersubjectivity differently. The limits of the individual are not a violent but a liminal space, a rich and curious dream world full of new possibilities, including perhaps the watching of animals instead of killing them. The end of the story, with the old man "dreaming about the lions," figures death not violently, as a trauma, but quietly, as a dream.

The lions certainly suggest the ferocity of appetite and of nature, but Santiago's dream lions "played like young cats in the dusk and he loved them as he loved the boy" (25). Perhaps some readers see this too as sentimental. But nature is more than merely "red in tooth and claw." In fact, lions do play as well as hunt, although our accounts of nature often override such ordinary realities to focus on dramas of life and death. This playful "dream" of nature haunts the story, quietly encouraging Santiago to move beyond the exigencies of hunger towards love for his ostensible adversary, the marlin. Santiago, like the later Hemingway, is a hunter who recognizes his place in his world, who knows that eating requires killing, but recognizes how much more there is to nature than killing.[8] In *The Old Man and the Sea*, this something more appears in all the textual details that reveal how much living contains the actual acts of killing and eating. The necessity of detail, the necessity of narrative itself, is evidence that the meaning of life cannot be reduced to simple death.

Santiago's utter exhaustion, caused by his protracted struggle with the fish and thus a physical acknowledgment of the fish, pushes his thinking another step: "There is no one worthy of eating him from the manner of his behavior and his great dignity." Nonetheless, Hemingway's narrative tells us that Santiago's "determination to kill [the fish] never relaxed in his sorrow for him" (*OMATS* 75). Across the fishing line, the marlin has interrupted Santiago's selfhood and exposed another fiction as fiction—that of commodity value. That is, commodity value is only one of many possible stories that we tell about something like a great fish. This point is reiterated both comically and dramatically once Santiago has killed the fish. Thinking that the marlin is "over fifteen hundred pounds" and wondering how much he is worth, Santiago says aloud, "'I need a pencil for that'" (97). And when the sharks hit, the gradual stripping of the marlin is recognized piece by piece; the mako shark, for example, takes "about forty pounds" (103).

This reckoning reduces the magnificent fish to pounds of meat, yet the whole story hinges on the unavoidable reality of animal appetite that drives Santiago, the marlin, and the sharks, a reality that prevents Santiago or Hemingway from freeing himself of such calculations. In other words, this story aims to show not only the majesty of the marlin, which makes its being eaten by sharks seem wasteful, but also the ordinary and universal fact of appetite. Death, at the center of this story and crucial to all appetite, can flatten hierarchies. A great fish, privileged in the story, becomes mere pounds of meat for sharks, and finally just one more piece of "garbage waiting to go out with the tide" (126). These losses of the marlin are practical, registered financially and in terms of the people the fish could feed, so that the irreducible beauty of this fish—the big one that could not be brought in—is coupled tightly to all ordinary animal needs. Such complexities prevent a simple ethical understanding and justify Santiago's nuanced sense that although killing some fish may be acceptable, killing this marlin was wrong: "'I shouldn't have gone out so far, fish,' he said. 'Neither for you nor for me. I'm sorry, fish'" (110).

With this full reading of *The Old Man and the Sea*, we can compare Hemingway's night walks in Africa to Santiago's self-condemnation. In a sense, when Toni Morrison accuses Hemingway of treating Africa as a "blank, empty space into which he asserts himself" (88–89), she is suggesting that Hemingway has, like Santiago, gone out too far. He has forced his way into another's identity. But Santiago's error can be more precisely located. It is not going too far out to sea or learning about the complexities of the wild ocean; it is trying to bring too much of that otherness back with him. The older Hemingway of *Under Kilimanjaro* shows greater restraint on this point, a restraint which appears in his hunting practices. During the spear-equipped night walk mentioned in opening this essay, for instance, Hemingway notices a wildebeest that he steers around. As he does so, he thinks, "I could always have killed the wildebeest, maybe [. . .]." He decides not to try because of the trouble of dealing with the animal responsibly after doing so; he would have to dress the body and then guard it against hyenas or "rouse the camp" like a "show-off" (*UK* 361). Additionally, few in the camp care for wildebeest meat. Hemingway's heedful decision conveys complex ethics that go beyond the simple application of an ethical rule.

The differences between going out and going out too far are important because they permit cross-cultural and inter-species exchange without necessarily rendering all such exchanges into imperialism or colonialism. They also demonstrate how simple ethical strictures can be misleading. Not only may what is right in one era prove wrong in another, and vice versa, but circumstances within an era may contradict its standard codes of ethical behavior. An ethical person must not only obey what seems to be a correct law, then; she or he must have a sensibility open to experiences which may themselves shift ethical thinking. Such a sensibility characterizes much of Hemingway's work, as it characterizes a book he greatly admired—Mark Twain's *The Adventures of Huckleberry Finn*. In one of the great ethical moments in American literature, Huck decides not to send the letter that would turn in the runaway slave Jim. Instead, Huck says, "'All right, then, I'll *go* to hell'" and tears the letter up (272; Ch. 31, original emphasis). In this case, as in much of Hemingway, Huck's own experience, his pleasant memories of Jim's goodness, lead him to contradict what the laws of the time and place dictate.

Ethics and Eating

Huck arrives at his decision after considerable brooding. Hemingway's work on hunting also demonstrates that what is ethical is not always obvious or simple. Attentive immersion in hunting restores the too-often-invisible complexity attending decisions about eating animals. Several critics, for instance, have helped us to see what was at issue historically in Santiago's fishing practice, which he takes to be more ethical than the younger men's methods. Hemingway briefly makes us aware of the other fishermen who use elaborate tools, "those who used buoys as floats for their lines and had motorboats, bought when the shark livers had brought much money [. . .]" (*OMATS* 29–30). Santiago chooses otherwise, holding to his simple implements.

Beegel argues that Santiago's approach to technology allows him "to uphold an ecological ethic diametrically opposed to Ahab's 'iron way'" ("Santiago and the Eternal Feminine" 143). She points out that the younger fishermen with all their gear "are the ancestors of today's long-liners" (143). Industrial fishing practices such as long-lining, with much larger catches than small-scale, traditional fishing practices such as Santiago's, are not only responsible for modern declines in marine populations, but have radically changed the culture of fishing among humans.[9] *The Old Man and the Sea* indicates the general mid-20th century shift towards using more technology but counters it with the lineage of Santiago and Manolin, demonstrating that cultural and technological questions may be more important ethically and ecologically than the sometimes reductive question about whether humans should ever kill animals. Nonetheless, the significance of each individual animal was also becoming more clear to Hemingway late in life.

The ethics and aesthetics of hunting, a form of engaged inhabitation of the world, attuned to the depths of self and the differences of others, was a locus of meaning in Hemingway's oeuvre. His later work expands on moments that appear in some of his earlier writing, especially the fishing stories. Those moments, such as the fishing interlude in *The Sun Also Rises*, are often read as providing some redemptive serenity in the midst of meaningless violence and confusion. Miriam B. Mandel, commenting on *Under Kilimanjaro*, suggests that Hemingway's quasi-fictional author-narrator still "needs (desperately, it seems to me) to construct some universal, comprehensive ethical system" (97). It is no accident that this desire manifests in a book centered on human/animal relationships in the radically different cultures and environment of East Africa. Hunting for principles to live by, for a religion of his own, was arguably Hemingway's lifelong undertaking, signs of which appear throughout his work, like tracks of some elusive animal. Our appetite for a universal ethics, however unappeasable, is itself perhaps the essence of the search for principles of right living. Hemingway's attentive, nuanced style reminds us that this desire for the universal must always be balanced against and informed by the details of the particular if we are to be ethical.

Works Cited

Baker, Carlos. *Ernest Hemingway: A Life Story*. New York: Scribner's, 1969.

Beegel, Susan F. "A Guide to the Marine Life in Ernest Hemingway's *The Old Man and the Sea*." Resources for American Literary Study 30 (2006): 236–315.

———. "Santiago and the Eternal Feminine: Gendering *La Mar* in *The Old Man and the Sea*." In *Hemingway and Women: Female Critics and the Female Voice*. Ed. Lawrence R. Broer and Gloria Holland. Tuscaloosa: U of Alabama P, 2002. 131–156.

Berger, James. "Falling Towers and Postmodern Wild Children: Oliver Sacks, Don Delillo, and Turns Against Language." *PMLA* 120.2 (2005): 341–361.

Bloom, Harold, ed. *Ernest Hemingway's The Old Man and the Sea*. Philadelphia, PA: Chelsea House, 1999.

———. Introduction. *Ernest Hemingway's The Old Man and the Sea*. Philadelphia, PA: Chelsea House, 1999. 1–3.

Burhans, Clinton S., Jr. "*The Old Man and the Sea*: Hemingway's Tragic Vision of Man." *American Literature* 31 (1960): 446–55. Rpt. in Bloom 45–52.

Burwell, Rose Marie. *Hemingway: The Postwar Years and the Posthumous Novels*. Cambridge, UK: Cambridge UP, 1996.

Clark, Suzanne. *Cold Warriors: Manliness on Trial in the Rhetoric of the West*. Carbondale, IL: Southern Illinois UP, 2000.

Davis, Todd F. and Kenneth Womack, eds. *Mapping the Ethical Turn: A Reader in Ethics, Culture, and Literary Theory*. Charlottesville, VA: UP of Virginia, 2001.

Derrida, Jacques. "And Say the Animal Responded?" In Wolfe, *Zoontologies* 121–146.

Del Gizzo, Suzanne. "Going Home: Hemingway, Primitivism, and Identity." *Modern Fiction Studies* 49.3 (2003): 496–523.

De Waal, Frans. *Primates and Philosophers: How Morality Evolved*. Princeton, NJ: Princeton UP, 2006.

Garber, Marjorie, Beatrice Hanssen, and Rebecca L. Walkowitz, eds. *The Turn to Ethics*. New York: Routledge, 2000.

Griffin, Donald R. *Animal Minds: Beyond Cognition to Consciousness*. Chicago, IL: U of Chicago P, 2001.

Harpham, Geoffrey Galt. "Ethics." In *Critical Terms for Literary Study*. 2nd ed. Ed. Frank Lentricchia and Thomas McLaughlin. Chicago, IL: U of Chicago P, 1995. 387–405.

Hauser, Marc D. *Moral Minds: How Nature Designed Our Universal Sense of Right and Wrong*. New York: Harper Collins, 2006.

Hemingway, Ernest. *The Complete Short Stories of Ernest Hemingway: The Finca Vigia Edition.* New York: Scribner's, 1987.

————. *Ernest Hemingway, Selected Letters: 1917–1961.* Ed. Carlos Baker. London: Granada, 1981.

————. *A Farewell to Arms.* New York: Scribner's, 1929.

————. *Green Hills of Africa.* New York: Scribner's, 1935.

————. *The Old Man and the Sea.* New York: Scribner's, 1952.

————. *The Sun Also Rises.* New York: Scribner's, 1926.

————. *True at First Light.* New York: Scribner's, 1999.

————. *Under Kilimanjaro.* Eds. Robert W. Lewis and Robert E. Fleming. Kent, OH: Kent State UP, 2005.

Jobes, Katharine T., ed. *Twentieth Century Interpretations of The Old Man and the Sea: A Collection of Critical Essays.* Englewood Cliffs, NJ: Prentice Hall, 1968.

Justus, James H. "The Later Fiction: Hemingway and the Aesthetics of Failure." In *Ernest Hemingway: New Critical Essays.* Ed. A. Robert Lee. London: Vision, 1983. 103–121. Rpt. in Bloom 125–139.

Lawlor, Leonard. *This Is Not Sufficient: An Essay on Animality and Human Nature in Derrida.* New York, NY: Columbia UP, 2007.

Lewis, Robert W. and Robert E. Fleming. Introduction. *Under Kilimanjaro.* Kent, OH: Kent State UP, 2005.

Levinas, Emmanuel. *Otherwise Than Being, Or Beyond Essence.* Trans. Alphonso Lingis. Pittsburgh, PA: Duquesne UP, 1998.

Love, Glen. "Hemingway's Indian Virtues: An Ecological Reconsideration." *Western American Literature* 22.3 (1987): 201–213.

Mandel, Miriam B. "Ethics and 'Night Thoughts': 'Truer than the Truth.'" *The Hemingway Review* 25.2 (Spring 2006): 95–100.

Murphy, Charlene M. "Hemingway's Gentle Hunters: Contradiction or Duality?" In *Hemingway and the Natural World*. Ed. Robert E. Fleming. Moscow, ID: U of Idaho P, 1999. 165–174.

Ondaatje, Christopher. *Hemingway in Africa: The Last Safari*. Woodstock: Overlook, 2004.

Rahv, Philip. Review. Commentary *14* (October 1952): 390–91. Rpt. in Robert O. Stephens. Ed. *Ernest Hemingway: The Critical Reception*. New York: Burt Franklin, 1977. 360–361.

Reynolds, Michael. *Hemingway: The Final Years*. New York: W.W. Norton, 1999.

Sylvester, Bickford. "The Cuban Context of *The Old Man and the Sea*." In The Cambridge Companion to Ernest Hemingway. Ed. Scott Donaldson. Cambridge, UK: Cambridge UP, 1996. 243–68.

———. "Hemingway's Extended Vision: *The Old Man and the Sea*." PMLA 81 (1966): 130–138. Rpt. in Jobes 81–96.

Trodd, Zoe. "Hemingway's Camera Eye: The Problem of Language and an Interwar Politics of Form." *The Hemingway Review* 26.2 (Spring 2007): 7–21.

Twain, Mark. *The Adventures of Huckleberry Finn*. 1884. New York: Harper, 1987.

Voeller, Carey. "'He Only Looked Sad the Same Way I Felt': The Textual Confessions of Hemingway's Hunters." *The Hemingway Review* 25.1 (Fall 2005): 63–76.

Wagner, Linda W., ed. *Ernest Hemingway: Six Decades of Criticism*. East Lansing, MI: Michigan State UP, 1987.

Weeks, Robert P. "Fakery in *The Old Man and the Sea*." *College English* 24 (1962): 188–192. Rpt. in Jobes 34–40.

Wolfe, Cary, ed. *Zoontologies: The Question of the Animal.* Minneapolis, MN: U of Minnesota P, 2003.

Young, Philip. *Ernest Hemingway: A Reconsideration.* University Park, PA: Pennsylvania State UP, 1966.

Ziff, Larzer. "The Social Basis of Hemingway's Style." *Poetics: International Review for the Theory of Literature* 7 (1978): 417–423. Rpt. in Wagner 147–154.

Notes

The author of this essay would like to thank Suzanne Clark for her incisive remarks on an earlier version.

1. Rose Marie Burwell corroborates this view, for instance. She explains that Hemingway's guide on his second African safari, Denis Zaphiro, reported Hemingway's preference for watching animals rather than killing them (137). Christopher Ondaatje also supports this characterization of Hemingway's second safari (see 179 for example), and Hemingway discusses his concerns with killing animals in his letters (e.g. SL 772).

2. The classic example is the dismissal of "abstract words" in *A Farewell to Arms* (184–185).

3. One debate between Levinas and Derrida is about whether to privilege the term "ethics." Derrida suggests not (see 121). For more on the ethical turn in theory, see James Berger's "Falling Towers and Postmodern Wild Children: Oliver Sacks, Don Delillo, and Turns against Language"; Todd F. Davis and Kenneth Womack's collection, *Mapping the Ethical Turn: A Reader in Ethics, Culture, and Literary Theory*, Marjorie Garber, Beatrice Hanssen, and Rebecca L. Walkowitz, who edited *The Turn to Ethics*; and Harpham's, "Ethics."

4. Leonard Lawlor's new book *This Is Not Sufficient: An Essay on Animality and Human Nature in Derrida* presents the notion of the "insufficiency" of systems of understanding, whether ethical or epistemological, as central to Derrida's philosophy, particularly his later texts on animals.

5. Beegel, in "A Guide to the Marine Life in Ernest Hemingway's *The Old Man and the Sea*," also remarks on how this passage shows that "Santiago clearly understands how the action of light on plankton changes the color of the sea" (284).

6. Robert Weeks makes this claim because of some factual errors he finds in the text. But Beegel's essay on the marine life in the book compellingly demonstrates not only how thorough Hemingway's general knowledge of the sea was, but also that Weeks's specific critiques of Hemingway are often wrong (see Beegel 276–

277, for example). Weeks goes on to claim that the story is "tricked out in an effort to extort more feeling than a reasonable person would find there" (40). This obviously gendered interpretive framework values the hard, scientific, manly writer in the science-oriented thinking of the cold war, but Hemingway was moving (even further) beyond that approach in this text. He was famously having some trouble taking this journey in the latter years, as he struggled to complete his many book projects (as Michael Reynolds's *Hemingway: The Final Years*, Carlos Baker's *Ernest Hemingway: A Life Story*, and other biographies report). We can imagine, however, why he may have experienced such difficulty in so polarized a critical environment. Suzanne Clark's *Cold Warriors: Manliness on Trial in the Rhetoric of the West* provides a full account of the critical climate in this period and a discussion of Hemingway's own difficulties. Another critique of *The Old Man and the Sea* can be found in James Justus, "The Later Fiction: Hemingway and the Aesthetics of Failure."

7. My reading here is indebted partly to Glen Love (207).

8. Much recent research has been conducted on the character of nature. See, for instance, Frans De Waal's *Primates and Philosophers*, where he argues that many of the elements of human morality are present in other animals, so that it is incorrect to understand nature as purely "red in tooth and claw." Other works along this line include Marc D. Hauser's *Moral Minds: How Nature Designed Our Universal Sense of Right and Wrong* and Donald R. Griffin's *Animal Minds: Beyond Cognition to Consciousness*.

9. In "The Cuban Context of The Old Man and the Sea," Bickford Sylvester also points to the sea-change in fishing practices occurring in the 1940s and 50s (e.g. 257).

Social Issues in Literature

Contemporary Perspectives on Death

Heavenly Fears of Dying

Dolores T. Puterbaugh

Dolores T. Puterbaugh, the American Thought Editor of USA Today Magazine, is a psychologist in private practice in Largo, Florida.

It is a natural human tendency to avoid the topic of death, states Dolores T. Puterbaugh in the following viewpoint. Although people profess a desire for a heavenly eternity, they don't want to go through the process of dying, she explains. This predilection reflects a basic tenant of human nature—while people are programmed to seek pleasure, they resist the pain and work involved in achieving it, she asserts.

Everyone wants to go to Heaven, but nobody wants to die. Elijah was taken there in a fiery chariot, but that's pretty much it. Even Jesus and His mother had to die before they were brought into Heaven, body and soul. The rest of us, apparently, also will have to die before meeting our final reward.

Most people spend a lot of time avoiding the idea of death. A friend has been fighting cancer for six years. She recently decided—enough. No more endless rounds of experimental chemotherapy and the resulting sickness. There is a window for some decent quality of life, and then she knows she will die. Her family is resisting—has been resisting—for years now. They do not want to face death, and if it means she has to suffer longer, that is a price they are prepared to let her pay.

Parents without wills or plans for their progeny think you are morbid if you suggest it might be prudent to make arrangements. Middle-aged people express surprise when someone as young as they inexplicably appears in the obituaries.

Dolores T. Puterbaugh, "Heavenly Fears of Dying," *USA Today Magazine*, vol. 139, no. 2788, January 2011, p. 82. Copyright © 2011 by USA Today Magazine. All rights reserved. Reproduced by permission.

Many elderly people, with long and rich lives, are reluctant to make the emotional and spiritual preparations necessary for psychological health at the end of life.

Coping with death is just one slice of the pie. Ease and bliss—a shallow feint at Heaven on earth—conflict with troublesome details, such as effort and sacrifice. Substance abuse, theft, and the epidemic bitterness encouraged against successful people are baser versions of the same desire: ecstasy without the agony. When then candidate Barack Obama suggested to Joe the Plumber that the fruits of Joe's labor ought to be "spread around" like orange marmalade on toast, there ought to have been a collective gasp sufficient to create a vacuum effect over the country. At least Mr. Obama was forthright about his intentions; many others harbor the same notion but have neither the weapons nor the personnel necessary to execute it.

Humans are programmed to seek pleasure. One of our neurotransmitters, dopamine, enjoys a particularly intimate relationship with thrills. Dopamine is part of the electrochemical charge of falling in love, winning at gambling, and excitement in general. The dopamine system evolves across the life span. Small children experience countless rushes—everything's wonderful! Snow! School! A snow day! Adults whose brains are unspoiled by drugs are barely moderated versions of children in this regard: Sunset! Sunrise! Sex! Steak! Cake! Teenagers, however, go through a phase where their dopamine systems, to put it crudely, either are flatlining or mainlining: Any experience is boring, boring, boooooring, or a complete high. This, plus brain changes related to executive function development, comprise a considerable source of the notorious stupidity of adolescence. The flat-line phenomenon is not unique to teens: Dopamine receptors are among several known neurotransmitters' receptors that can be burned out by stimulants such as Ritalin, other amphetamines, and cocaine. Possibly, many drug abusers suffer actual chemical ennui due

It is a natural human tendency to avoid the topic of death. Although people profess a desire for a heavenly eternity, they don't want to go through the process of dying. © Mopic/ Alamy.

to neural exhaustion and neurotransmitter depletion. The end result, however, speaks to the preliminary problem of wanting a thrill without working for it.

Change requires rewiring the brain—literally. Learning may occur in a single event, but generally the hardwiring of neural development is slower. If the desired change provokes temper tantrums in the pleasure-seeking dopamine system, it is prudent to plan for roadblocks, setbacks, and the interference of those near and dear to us. It is an essential strategy, because brain physiology and chemistry often are set up in opposition to change, even change that is good for us.

An acquaintance recently remarked that it was time to get religious about his health. He is not atypical: He fancies himself too busy to eat properly, although not too busy to eat out most nights. A normal schedule justifies insufficient time for consistent exercise, etc. Implicit assumptions bespoke trouble. First was the apparent perception that making new choices was something static: that the better choices made at 39 would suit at 49, 60, or 75. He seemed oblivious to the many variables linked to the behavior he wanted to change. What friendships revolve around dining out or a few beers after work? What daily conversations concern the television shows he will miss if he spends an hour at the gym? Who—romantic partner, cat, or employer—will feel cheated if he carves out time for his new routine? He was unprepared for the fluidity of life and the challenges that make psychological shock absorbers so helpful. Finally, one of the high-grade psychological shock absorbers—accepting that emotions sometimes merely are marginally interesting information, not a compass—was missing. Being committed to an exercise program does not cause one to "feel like" rolling out of bed for a run in the sleet. At some point, the "feeling" must be treated as little more than a buzzing mosquito in the panoply of brain activity.

He envisions grocery shopping and cooking fresh meals from scratch but, without strategies to cope with subtle details, change will be more excruciating than necessary. He either will learn to keep a running list of items for grocery shopping, or shop nearly daily. The latter is as much a time killer as dining out can be. Cooking sounds good until the night that either takeout or a bowl of cereal over the sink are the best options because it has been a hellish day and what he planned last weekend intersects with working three hours late on Wednesday night. Then there is the appestat adjustment: a grilled chicken breast and crisp green salad are not as filling as a burger and fries. Hunger, or a lack of fullness, will be one of his new friends. That is good; he will need friends. His other friends will gripe because he's never around; they will make plans without him; eventually, he will have to choose between workouts and his social circle.

We cannot experience true life without acknowledging death. Childbirth is painful; meaningful friendships require effort; and a rich spiritual life takes time, too. We resist facing the inevitable: Bliss requires suffering. Everyone wants to go to Heaven, but nobody wants to die.

A Grudge Match Between Humanity and Death—Who Wins?

Mason Media Blog

Mason Media Blog *is the blog of George Mason University.*

In the following viewpoint, the Mason Media Blog *reports on the research of George Mason University psychology professor Todd Kashdan on the effects of being a mindful person. Kashdan defines mindful people as those who are open and receptive to what is happening in the present. In his research, Kashdan determined that mindful people are less fearful of death and more tolerant of others.*

Death can be terrifying. Recognizing that death is inescapable and unpredictable makes us incredibly vulnerable, and can invoke feelings of anxiety, hatred and fear. But new research by George Mason University psychology professor Todd Kashdan shows that being a mindful person not only makes you generally more tolerant and less defensive, but it can also actually neutralize fears of dying and death.

"Mindfulness is being open, receptive, and attentive to whatever is unfolding in the present moment," says Kashdan. In his latest research, Kashdan and his colleagues wanted to find out if mindful people had different attitudes about death and dying.

"Generally, when reminded of our mortality, we are extremely defensive. Like little kids who nearly suffocate under blanket protection to fend off the monster in the closet, the first thing we try to do is purge any death-related thoughts or feelings from our mind," says Kashdan.

"On the fringes of this conscious awareness, we try another attempt to ward off death anxiety. We violently defend beliefs and practices that provide a sense of stability and meaning in our lives."

Kashdan says this practice often has an ugly side—intolerance and abuse. "When people are reminded that death is impending, their racist tendencies increase," he says. In a series of experiments conducted by the University of Missouri-Columbia, for example, white people asked to read about a crime committed by another person give harsher penalties for black compared with white defendants after being reminded of their mortality.

Kashdan wondered what might prevent these defensive, intolerant reactions from occurring. In a recent study published in the *Journal of Personality and Social Psychology*, he and his colleagues looked at what might happen when mindfulness and the terror of death collide.

"A grudge match between humanity and death," says Kashdan.

If mindful people are more willing to explore whatever happens in the present, even if it is uncomfortable, will they show less defensiveness when their sense of self is threatened by a confrontation with their own mortality?

Based on the results of 7 different experiments, the answer appears to be yes. When reminded about their death and asked to write about what will happen when their bodies decompose (in grisly detail), less mindful people showed an intense dislike for foreigners that mention what's wrong with the United States (pro-U.S. bias), greater prejudice against black managers who discriminated against a white employee in a promotion decision (pro-white bias), and harsher penalties for social transgressions such as prostitution, marital infidelities, and drug use by physicians that led to surgical mishaps.

Across these various situations, on the contrast, *mindful* people showed a lack of defensiveness toward people that didn't share their worldview. Mindful people were diplomatic and tolerant regardless of whether they were prompted to think about their slow, systematic decline toward obliteration.

"What we found was that when asked to deeply contemplate their death, mindful people spent more time writing (as opposed to avoiding) and used more death-related words when reflecting on the experience. This suggests that a greater openness to processing the threat of death allows compassion and fairness to reign. In this laboratory-staged battle, mindfulness alters the power that death holds over us," Kashdan says.

Should You Fear Death?

Paul Thagard

Paul Thagard is a Canadian philosopher who specializes in cognitive science and the philosophy of science. He is a professor of psychology and the director of the cognitive science program at the University of Waterloo as well as the author of numerous books.

In this viewpoint, Paul Thagard declares that the argument of ancient Greek philosopher Epicurus against the fear of death remains true today. Epicurus claimed that there is no reason to fear death because a person ceases to exist at the point of death and therefore has no experience of pleasure or pain. Thagard cites contemporary neuroscience in support of Epicurus's argument.

Many psychologists have asserted that people are heavily motivated by fear of their own mortality. This claim may well describe large numbers of people, not just Woody Allen, but is it normatively correct? Is it rational to fear death? How might this philosophical question be given an evidence-based answer?

It is still commonly believed that being rational is at odds with being emotional, but emotions such as fear can often be quite reasonable. For example, if a hurricane is predicted in the area in which you live, it is rational to fear the damage that can result, and evidence is accumulating to support fears about drastic declines in the environment resulting from climate change. On the other hand, fear about some potential event is irrational when there is no evidence that the event will actually threaten a person's well-being. Developing a strong fear of the earth being hit by a huge asteroid is currently irrational because there is no evidence that an asteroid strike is imminent. Is death like the hurricane or like the asteroid strike?

More than two thousand years ago, the Greek philosopher Epicurus constructed an argument against fearing death that has since become even more plausible: "Death does not concern us, because as long as we exist, death is not here. And when it does come, we no longer exist." Epicurus was one of the first atomists who believed that everything consists of material entities and that there are no souls that survive death. If your life ends at death, then you have nothing to fear, because there will be no *you* to experience pleasure or pain. It's all over when it's over.

Of course, there are other aspects of dying that are worth fearing, such as disease, disability, and the distress of people who care about you. But from the philosophical perspective that there is no life after death, death itself is nothing to fear.

Especially in recent decades, evidence has mounted that Epicurus was right that minds are material processes rather than supernatural souls. Cognitive neuroscience is rapidly developing experiments and theories that support the claim that the identification of mind and brain provides the best explanation of people's capacities for perception, reasoning, language, and even consciousness. If the mind is just the brain, then there is no mind to experience suffering of any kind when the brain stops functioning at death. Hence Epicurus was right that there is nothing to fear. If there were any good evidence that life does survive death, then we would have to reject Epicurus's conclusion, but phenomena such as near-death experiences and séances can easily be explained away.

The fear of death persists as a vestige of religious views that proclaim that life on earth is just a fragment of the existence of an eternal soul. Then religion becomes a solution to a problem that it has itself created: You may be able to decrease

The Greek philosopher Epicurus believed there was no reason to fear death because a person ceases to exist at the point of death and therefore has no experience of pleasure or pain. © Bettmann/Corbis.

your fear of death by believing that you have found the right religion that will ensure that your afterlife will be pleasant. Thus religion allows a person to careen from the fear-driven inference that death is threatening to the motivated inference that it won't be so bad in the afterlife. Of course, this inference assumes that you have picked the right religion.

If I believed that life survives death, then I would be terrified at the prospect of an eternity of suffering, because I would have no way of knowing which religious beliefs to adopt. In addition to the different main religions such as Christianity, Islam, Hinduism, Buddhism, and Judaism, there are many variants, including dozens of different versions of Catholicism, Protestantism, and Islam. Guessing wrong could lead not only to problems in this life, but also to eternal punishment. Moreover, it is entirely possible that the "right" religion hasn't even been invented yet.

This variety is one of the flaws in Pascal's famous wager that it is better to believe in God, because if religion turns out to be true, then you get eternal reward, instead of suffering eternal punishment. This wager assumes that you know what religion to bet on. In contrast, let me offer Thagard's wager: It is better not to believe in God, because then you don't have to suffer through a lifetime of worrying about death and the right religion! Happily, this wager fits perfectly with rapidly developing evidence that the mind is just the brain. Hence both inference to the best explanation and inference to the best plan support the conclusion that death should not be feared.

Fear of Aging Can Cause Behavior That Results in Death

Lauren E. Popham, Sheila M. Kennison, and Kristopher I. Bradley

Lauren E. Popham is with the Department of Psychology of North Carolina State University. Sheila M. Kennison is an associate professor of psychology at Oklahoma State University. Kristopher I. Bradley is a National Science Foundation fellow at Oklahoma State University.

Research shows that young people who fear death and old age are more prone to engage in risky behaviors, Lauren E. Popham, Sheila M. Kennison, and Kristopher I. Bradley report in the following viewpoint. They theorize that a fear of death may make teens more apt to engage in activities that enhance their sense of strength and invulnerability, and these typically are risky behaviors. The authors also suggest that programs aimed at reducing ageism and anxiety about aging may result in reducing risk-taking behaviors.

Risk-taking in adolescents and young adults is a major public health issue, not only because of the link between risk-taking and mortality, but also because of the cost to society. Prior research has identified a variety of factors associated with risk-taking by adolescents and young adults, including personal characteristics. For example, the persistent desire for stimulating, novel experiences has been found to be a strong predictor of risk-taking. The term sensation-seeking has been used to describe this trait. A growing body of literature sug-

Lauren E. Popham, Sheila M. Kennison, and Kristopher I. Bradley, "Ageism, Sensation-Seeking, and Risk-Taking Behavior in Young Adults," *Current Psychology*, vol. 30, 2011, pp. 184–86, 190. Copyright © 2011 by Springer. All rights reserved. Reproduced with kind permission from Springer Science+Business Media B.V.

gests there are biological correlates associated with sensation-seeking. In contrast, recent research shows that social factors are also related to risk-taking. [Lauren E.] Popham et al. found that young adults reporting more negative attitudes about aging and more ageist behaviors were found to engage in more risk-taking than those reporting less negative attitudes about aging and fewer ageist behaviors. The present research examined further the extent to which ageism and sensation-seeking are related to risk-taking in young adults. . . .

The purpose of the present research was to investigate an alternate view of risk-taking, one that involves social processes. The present research extends recent work by Popham et al. that showed that there is a link between ageism and risk-taking in young adults. In a study involving 408 participants, they confirmed the hypothesis, showing that as ageist attitudes and behaviors increased, so did risk-taking behaviors, particularly behaviors related to sexual activity, drinking, tobacco use, and drug abuse. The results were consistent with the view that young people may buffer their death anxiety by engaging in activities that make them feel strong, energetic, and invulnerable (i.e., experiences involving risk-taking). Furthermore, those with positive views of aging may avoid risk, because they desire to live as long as possible; the preservation of the physical body is essential to achieving old age.

Popham et al.'s results add to the growing number of studies supporting terror management theory. Terror management theory grew out of work by the cultural anthropologist Ernest Becker, who recognized fear of mortality as an important element of human psychology. Terror management theory proposes that individuals buffer their death anxiety by obtaining self-esteem from their culture. One way in which young people may try to buffer their death anxiety is by distancing themselves from their future, older selves by stereotyping and stigmatizing older people. . . .

The purpose of the present study was to investigate the extent to which both ageism and sensation-seeking predict risk-taking behavior in young adults. We hypothesized that both ageism and sensation-seeking would be related to risk-taking behavior. We also considered the alternative hypothesis that ageism, when measured in the same study with sensation-seeking, would account for variance in addition to that accounted for by sensation-seeking. . . .

The present research replicated the previous findings of Popham et al. in that there is a link between ageism and risk-taking by young adults. Those reporting engaging in more ageist behaviors also reported taking more risks in daily life. The present results also confirmed prior research showing that two dimensions of sensation-seeking—disinhibition and experience-seeking—were related to risk-taking. Higher levels of disinhibition and experience-seeking were related to higher levels of risk-taking. Most importantly, we found that in a hierarchical regression, when holding sensation-seeking constant, ageist behavior was a significant and unique predictor of risk-taking. Individuals reporting higher amounts of ageist behavior engaged in more risk-taking. We did not find ageist attitudes to be a significant predictor of risk-taking; however, ageist attitudes were significantly correlated with disinhibition.

The results have implications for how educators and policy makers might attempt to reduce risk-taking in adolescents and young adults. Programs could be developed to educate young people about the realities of aging, specifically the fact that aging can be a positive experience. Future research may be able to show that programs that reduce fear of aging in young adults may have the added benefit of also reducing their risk-taking in daily life. There is some preliminary data suggesting that individuals' views of aging can be modified. [Linda J.] Allan and [James A.] Johnson found that higher levels of knowledge about aging reduced anxiety about aging, which in turn reduced ageist attitudes. Their results supported the view that programs aimed at reducing ageism should focus on reducing the anxiety about aging rather than focusing solely on disseminating factual knowledge about aging.

For Further Discussion

1. Many writers including John C. Unrue and Robert Roper write about Hemingway's self-destructive tendencies, suggesting that he courted death throughout his life. What were some of the ways in which Hemingway endangered himself? Do you believe he was self-destructive or adventuresome? Explain your answer.

2. Several critics including Daniel Listoe, Stanley Cooperman, and William E. Cain write about the similarities between Hemingway and Santiago. In what ways are they similar and in what ways do they differ? Explain using examples from the viewpoints presented.

3. Although Santiago is unsuccessful in bringing the giant marlin to shore, most critics write about the old fisherman's moral victory. Do you agree that Santiago is victorious despite his defeat? Why?

4. In chapter 3, the *Mason Media Blog* reports on research that indicates that people who are "mindful," that is, open to life, are less likely to be fearful of dying. Do you consider Santiago to be a mindful person? Cite examples of his openness and acceptance of life.

5. Lauren E. Popham, Sheila M. Kennison, and Kristopher I. Bradley have conducted research showing that young people who fear death and old age are more prone to engage in risky behaviors. Do you feel the life of Hemingway lends support to their theory? If so, how? Explain.

For Further Reading

Albert Camus, *The Stranger*. New York: Knopf, 1946.

Ernest Hemingway, *A Farewell to Arms*. New York: Scribner, 1929.

————, *Islands in the Stream*. New York: Scribner, 1970.

————, *A Moveable Feast*. New York: Scribner, 1964.

————, *To Have and Have Not*. New York: Scribner, 1937.

Rudyard Kipling, *Captains Courageous: A Story of the Grand Banks*. New York: Century Co., 1897.

Jack London, *The Sea-Wolf*. London: Heinemann, 1904.

Herman Melville, *Moby-Dick; or The Whale*. New York: Harper & Brothers, 1851.

John Steinbeck, *Of Mice and Men*. New York: Covici-Friede, 1937.

————, *The Pearl*. New York: Viking, 1947.

Mark Twain, *The Adventures of Huckleberry Finn*. New York: Charles L. Webster and Company, 1885.

Bibliography

Books

Gerry Brenner   *The Old Man and the Sea: Story of a
                    Common Man.* New York: Twayne,
                    1991.

Douglas J. Davies   *A Brief History of Death.* Malden,
                    MA: Wiley-Blackwell, 2005.

Scott Donaldson,   *The Cambridge Companion to
ed.   Hemingway.* New York: Cambridge
                    University Press, 1996.

Andrea Fontana   *Death and Dying in America.* Malden,
and Jennifer Reid   MA: Polity Press, 2009.
Keene

Norberto Fuentes   *Hemingway in Cuba.* Secaucus, NJ:
                    Lyle Stuart, 1984.

Peter L. Hays   *Ernest Hemingway.* New York:
                    Continuum, 1990.

Mary Welsh   *How It Was.* New York: Knopf, 1976.
Hemingway

James Nagel, ed.   *Ernest Hemingway: The Writer in
                    Context.* Madison: University of
                    Wisconsin Press, 1984.

Michael Reynolds   *Hemingway: The Final Years.* New
                    York: Norton, 1999.

Earl Rovit   *Ernest Hemingway.* New York:
                    Twayne, 1963.

Delbert E. Wylder   *Hemingway's Heroes.* Albuquerque:
University of New Mexico Press,
1969.

Periodicals

Clinton S.
Burhans Jr.

"*The Old Man and the Sea*:
Hemingway's Tragic Vision of Man,"
American Literature, January 1960.

Geoffrey Dow

"Mortality," *Humanist Perspectives*,
Winter 2012.

F.W. Dupee

"Hemingway Revealed," *Kenyon
Review*, Winter 1953.

Charles K.
Hofling

"Hemingway's *The Old Man and the
Sea* and the Male Reader," *American
Imago*, Summer 1963.

Milton Howard

"Hemingway and Heroism," *Masses
and Mainstream*, October 1952.

Stephen Marche

"Aren't We Enjoying All This
Celebrity Death a Little Too Much?,"
Esquire, December 2009.

Philip Melling

"Cultural Imperialism, Afro-Cuban
Religion, and Santiago's Failure in
Hemingway's *The Old Man and the
Sea*," *Hemingway Review*, Fall 2006.

Donna M.
Nickitas

"The Dialogue About Death and
Dying: It's Time," *Nursing Economics*,
May–June 2012.

Mark Schorer

"With Grace Under Pressure," *New
Republic*, October 6, 1952.

Will Self	"The Suburban Way of Death," *New Statesman*, January 16, 2012.
Robert O. Stephens	"Hemingway's Old Man and the Iceberg," *Modern Fiction Studies*, Winter 1961–62.
Ove G. Svensson	"Ernest Hemingway and the Nobel Prize for Literature," *Hemingway Review*, Spring 2008.
Charles Taylor	"*The Old Man and the Sea*: A Nietzschean Tragic Vision," *Dalhousie Review*, Winter 1981–82.
Eric Waggoner	"Inside the Current: A Taoist Reading of *The Old Man and the Sea*," *Hemingway Review*, Spring 1998.
Will Wlizlo	"Fifty Years Without Hemingway," *Utne Reader*, July 2011.

Index